NO FAULT

(New Opportunities for Amazing Unusual Leadership Transformation)

A Journey in Servant Leadership

———————

Porsha M. Stubbs

NO FAULT
Copyright © 2023 by Porsha M. Stubbs

ISBN: 979-8-218-35385-8

Acknowledgment
To my family,
Vanis, Rudolph, Jefre, Courtnee and Kevin, and
granddaughters Cobrianna and Reagan
THANK YOU!

"If the first covenant had been faultless, there would have been no need for a second covenant to replace it. Hebrews 8: 7~NLT

Contents

INTRODUCTION

"We are hard pressed on every side, but not crushed; perplexed, but not in despair". II Corinthians 4:8.

Since March 2020, the height of the COVID-19 pandemic, the coronavirus brought society to a screeching halt, transforming the way we all previously knew life. Every society and community were on coronavirus lock down, (COVID-19) forcing a global shift to conform, transform, and pivot systems and cultures. If your choice were abstinence, rest assured in time you would have to face the consequences of not giving into change. The volumes of my life can be referenced to COVID- 19, as in every season be it politics, personal, or prescriptive the times demanded conformity or isolation. The protocols of this era were not clear to those whose roles demanded their response for the safety of others. In most of the seasons, the pain experienced felt like the clichés, "pressure bursts pipe", and "pressure punishes procrastination" making an impactful bolster to the mindset. During each season I was under conviction to use the free time wisely; do something constructive that hopefully would result in GOOD eventually.

That lock down turned out to be the impetus I needed in 2020 to reflect on my quality of life. I enrolled in a doctoral program, at Regent University, Virginia, USA even though, the world was falling apart, and I had two failed attempts at beginning a doctoral program, only completing the first semester, at the University of West Indies, "Go Pelicans," a top-tier educational system in the Caribbean and Latin America. I just knew it was time and since I am a forward thinker, I prefer to be prepared no matter which side the pendulum swings. Society as we knew it halted, and virtual employment increased. Ideas froze and activities lay dormant, while innovations leaped. Concrete walls, as the world was accustomed to, pivoted into personal space, "virtual" or work from home. Working from home exposed all my deficiencies and increased many anxiety levels. Nevertheless, despite the norms being shaken and human emotions multiplying, the work and progress had to continue. People who were dreamers became creators and innovators, while educational pursuits blossomed.

Looking back, that time and season made me reflect on my personal and professional life, for certainly the reality of an empty calendar was extremely daunting. Every vacant slot showed that I had more than enough time to spare and could do more. I had more time than usual and challenged us all to become more familiar with all aspects of technology, social media, and e-platforms, as these forms of communication were unlimited. Governing at that time was the responsibility of the ruling party, the People's Democratic Movement, of which I was not a part. In contrast, traditional politicking ceased and the workload of the Opposition, the Progressive National Party, consisted of more verbal advocacy than actual physical work. Times were different, change was clear, era was new, and growth was undeniable.

New eras call for growth, development, and maturation. Maturation stages in humanity stem from womb to the tomb[1], and in each life cycle there are bumps and bruises on each level and tiers of tests and trials. Humans are stretched at every level of

---

[1] (Piaget, 1932)

competence, just like in a court trial, there is always a verdict. Over time every obstacle that I have had to face lifted my emotions, body, and fiscal contribution, without calculation in most instances and often with the end results acting as ignition to moving me forward. Every course in the obstacle supplied both anxiety and motivation which propelled me to move and not worry about landing on my feet. Fast forward to this time and the writing of this book, I understand that I was in all aspects a leader, being crushed, yet being trained to what I knew as being a transformational/ servant leader.

From childhood to adulthood, the seasons changed and so did the people who helped me. Each rung in the ladder required more and each season difficult for me to navigate through the experiences, negative or positive, that shaped my influence or experience. The limited examples of leadership that I saw came from my parents, the most outstanding human servant leaders I know, from suffering horrible abuse from the time they were born. Both persevered in trials and tests after having begun a family of their own. My father was a warrior naturally and physically, and my mom was a warrior in the spirit, depending on God to supernaturally move in her defense, which He did many times for her. Constantly, she thanked God for protecting her family from plots and schemes of people whose interests toward us were evil.

In each stage, I faced battles, but there were angels assigned to help me through them. I thank my parents and many volunteers for engaging me in programs and initiatives that taught me the values of being empathetic, compassionate, community oriented, as well as the value of being a good steward. The volunteers created avenues for my growth and development by enabling me to become an excellent communicator and by entrusting me with leadership responsibilities at an early age – Girls Brigade and church were my fix.

The relationships, careers, business ventures and employment opportunities I chose were just avenues to purpose. One of my most memorable career moments was becoming a banker and a temporary lead pastor. Also, for a short while, I was a gatekeeper for an attorney that journey, one for the books. However, if you know me well, you know that taking orders is like me having an allergic outbreak, but they all fit well in the plan God had for my life. I am a control freak and my pain at various pit stops proves who I was designed to be. I see myself in Romans 12: 8, *"If your gift is to encourage others, be encouraging. If it is giving, give generously. If God has given you leadership ability, take the responsibility seriously. And if you have a gift of showing kindness to others, do it gladly."* (NLT)

Pain is cyclical and abuse is often looked at as only physical yet having many categories; one not often addressed is fiscal responsibility. Money management is essential to ensuring a prosperous financial future. God gives us the ability to create and get wealth, and too often our facilitation of it causes us to stray from achieving meaningful goals. As individuals, we are charged with properly handling what we are to steward. Whether in communities on social issues or mingling with the wealthy, access to financial means and information is still limited. The desire to obtain wealth should never be a priority until you understand its power (Hebrews 13:5). Despite my focus, family was and still is my wealth. I want wealth, while having the love of family but I remain hungry toward the fiscal.

Participation in the governance of a country comes in two phases – before and after the campaign. Campaigning was fun, politicking was stressful, and governance, the highest learning curve I ever achieved in my life, introduced me to tiers of strengths I never imagined I had. Each of these elements allowed me to strive not only for myself, but for others who aligned themselves through my political representation. This level was different from college, where I grew to appreciate advocacy, and the networking that this level of activism created. In college I was able to introduce myself to the world as a leader, and represented students whose concerns would not be heard otherwise. Not so in leading a country (politricks) where this kind of escalation required many tricks and prayers.

Leadership was in action, far from being just a buzz word in all sides of my life's journey. Never more than a mention here or there, essentially because once you are identified as leader the expectations increase from those around you. No sooner than I had identified with what I was being transformed into, did I realize that I was "made for more." So, in humility, obedience on my part (amid tears, and plenty of them), I placed my hand in God's hands, and his calculations, measurements, and formulas were just what I needed in each season. The extraction of formative ideals, practices, and a transformation to those of us who are seeking a life filled with gratitude and joy. Contextually in the theory of leadership this process highlights the attributes of the follower, living a life of expectation and desire to change igniting the posture of servant leadership with NO FAULT!

LEADERSHIP

"Unless the LORD builds the house, its builders labor in vain.

Unless the LORD watches over the city, the watchmen stand guard

in vain," Psalms 127:1.

Becoming and existing as a leader is a sacrificial workout. Leaders are change agents and the expectation from most is that they model when the goal is to influence others. Unfortunately, some individuals only see leadership as a resource to [2]improve their personal agendas. Despite how leadership is viewed, each concept has proven that no single type of leadership approach is best suited for every individual. The strength and weakness of leadership weighs heavily on the response of those they lead be it teams or individuals according to leadership texts and research.

According to [3] Burns motivate leaders to extend themselves beyond what they are accustomed to, causing them to think creatively and elevate their standards for the good of the community,

---

[2] (Northouse, 2019)

[3] (Burns, 1978)

organization, and team. It is vital for Leader's to value followers' morals and values and consider them to be a key factor in decision making and remain aware of risks that may be associated. There is no room for tolerance in governance but extreme fair play in good leadership.

Communication is vital to successful leadership. Pastoring as a leader is like leading in politics except it was my job to persuade them that a relationship with Jesus was more tangible than what I could offer as the people's representative. Immediately my thoughts went to, 1 Timothy 4:1 paraphrased, *"it is important for me to watch how I live and what I teach, being truthful, and stick to what is right for the sake of my testimony and the testimony of others"*.

Unfortunately, while politics and governance are to be referred to as the same, they are not. Potential candidates and elected officials find that these roles are vastly different and require distinct levels of aptitude like that of workout. In each tier of exercising accountability increases and with no formal training either is often left alone to face the cry or concern of voters and the feeling of being inadequate and undervalued can rise to a level of overwhelming.

The expectation based on the vote cast carries the weight of assuming the position of voters' personal and fiscal counsellor. These include car notes, house rent, groceries, shopping spree, contracts awarded, and the list is unlimited. No money, no vote, no concessions, no vote, no appearance during the tenure in office, no vote. While those whose tenure in politics are aware of these traits being forewarned is not something that is eagerly shown. The role of the candidate in achieving this is of no concern to the party. This to a candidate can be extremely overwhelming.

Depression kicked in, could you believe it? Such exhaustion reminded me of the response my father gave when he learned that I was given an opportunity to further my education at tertiary level. While he believed I was going to be successful the process of getting there was not his responsibility. I was already a *"mother/parent,"* his exact words, "you are a parent, and parents don't excel beyond that of being a parent." Although others saw my strengths and weakness and, in some instances threats, lacking was the support of my parents (father) who saw the opportunity which motivated me to continue pursuing a tertiary level education not profitable at that time. He declared he would stand on the sidelines and clap me over the finish line but that was as far as he was willing to go.

Parenting was my present, not my destiny nor my goal. As a politician I won, and I served in the first four years as Minister of Home Affairs, Health and Human Services, and Tourism Environment Culture and Heritage. The growth and development that was experienced during this season caused me to understand the purpose of leadership and the value of followers. The emphasis that had to be placed on constituents aligned with the goals of being an above average performer as a politician/representative. Primary to all aspects of politics is the fact that constituents are your boss, plain and simple which means that you can have anywhere from 1 to 1300 bosses: each unique in needs, and peculiar in desires.

Pastoring was new to me. It was a role that I was thrust into, and unenviable to me in every sense of the word. Pastors are shepherds, who care for the wellbeing of their sheep through scriptural, instruction, and modeling. Often, we speak about standing in the gap for an individual, not understanding that the spoken and the actions are as far as the directions, and according to Jeremiah 23:1 *"sorrows await them"*.

As humans our experience with most things are novice until it happens to us. My pastor passed away, and the church lacked the structure to continue creating room for unplanned events. A responsibility that is as colorful as politics, and as taxing as not taking care of your body, which can result in a terminal disease, and you die as a result.

In an essay penned by a researcher[4] on the historical books, in his examination of the leadership transition from Moses to Joshua he listed ten attributes one can use to identify when considering their roles as leaders: Leadership is a gift as well as a commission from God; what I went through to be prepared are just tactical training for the journey. As a leader is prepared, he transitions to becoming a servant – the promotion of trust is found in this ideology. Leadership shaping will cause you to have personal encounters with God. The act of being confident as a leader does not omit your submission to the plan and purpose of God. Leaders are dependent on the promises

---

[4] (Moskala, 2014)

19

of God. Leaders are to model values and principles. Followers want to be assured that their leader is accountable. Leaders must have an unobstructed vision of the task and goal. Leaders must have courage in difficulty and be able to progress in adversity. Leaders must be meditators, constantly seeking guidance from God, the wise one as they transcend.

Leadership without love is leadership that is form, fashion, and the non-existence of power. Love [5]historically does not make the cut when one is considering leadership attributes; however, to do so one must embrace what love can do, and how love transforms while leading. Love is an instrument, and it provokes leadership to support balance and implore wisdom. Love acts, supplies ability, and relates. [6]Collectively from the early 1900's to the present, the definition of leadership continues to evolve. Despite the various thoughts and ideas on what leadership is, the impact of leadership is wrapped in love. To explain, even though my roles as a parent, politician, and pastor gave me power and

---

[5] (Ricciardi, 2014)
[6] (Northouse, 2019)

presence only two of the three of them required me to have the capacity to love.

An unnecessary evil in leadership is not recognizing that you are a leader. Having a desire to serve and lead complicates whether such a decision would land you in spaces where you are surviving instead of thriving. Complex in many situations that I faced, still my earnest desire was to become a change agent for what was present in my space. Poverty was a common denominator throughout the entire process, and the only way out was to become a servant, while leading. My approach early on was not made up initially with love, but disdain and anger. I soon learned that LOVE was the key to unlocking, unleashing, and uniting those who I intended to lead.

Servant leadership, an approach in leadership was first formulated by Greenleaf who got the idea by reading a story by [7]Herman Hess called "Journey to the East." Many of us tasked with such a mantle do not understand nor have all the answers when we begin to [8]feel the unnatural desire to "serve," rather than lead. I

---

[7] (Hess, 1956) (Northouse, 2019)
[8] (Greenleaf, 1991, 2008)

know for certain that was my experience. When I was asked to lead a church, I accepted it with clear instructions that no one call me "Interim Pastor, or Pastor". When I was elected to Parliament, I often accepted people calling me by my first name instead of "Honorable Porsha Stubbs." When I led teams in organizations, I hated the word/s, "Boss, Boss lady, and Manager."

Servant leaders are not intrigued with power but are emboldened to bring about mindset and cultural change for the good of all. The gospel according to Mark 10: 43, states "...*Instead, whoever wants to become great among you must be your servant, and whoever wants to be first must be slave of all.*" Slavery in this age is completely unnecessary, and the thought of becoming enslaved is appalling. Not exactly my idea when reflecting on the characteristics of a servant leader but in truth my experience. So, with the protection of God's hand and the Holy Spirit supplying directions, correction, and peace, I made it. God worked in me and through me while I learned to Listen, Empathize, Heal, have Awareness, use Persuasion, have Conceptualization, Foresight, Stewardship, Commitment to the growth of people, and groomed in skills needed for Building community. I am not ashamed of my past; I am grateful that he chose me.

NEW

"So, God created mankind in his own image, in the image of God he created them; male and female he created them". Genesis 1:27

Nature

The practice of invoking God's presence into my life and situations came naturally and it was indicative of how I started each life lesson leaning on faith. I learned how to pray from two of my favorite strong ladies, my grandmothers, one I called "Gramma" and the other "Grandmother." My grandmothers were strong, and their husbands allowed them to explore their leadership potential. Increasingly faith was a pillar resident in my life, and often I became annoyed with the prescription that faith infused even though it was modeled. I often lacked the will to conform to faith principles and preferred the promotion of my independence.

Both of my grandmothers, Rose, and Lillian were consistent prayer warriors. It seemed as if they conspired about what they chose to instill in their families and they were very instrumental in the methods used to ensure that God was at the center of our homes and lives. Why? How? They bore a striking resemblance to each other in rituals and practices. Rose and Lillian without fail and especially on weekends woke their families up for prayer at 5 a.m. Whether it was Grand Bahama, New Providence, Bahamas or Providenciales, Turks and Caicos Islands my brother and I (the oldest grandchildren) knew two things for sure, and one for certain that we were going to sleep in the middle of our grandparents every night, and on weekends we were going to be awakened by our grandparents for 5 a.m. prayer with the rest of the family.

From this ritual, an important characteristic had been instilled in me, humility, and attitude toward prayer. I became an avid talker to God in his ears and practiced a daily relationship with him. One such example most recently occurred in March 2020. I put my mouth to action, and in an exercise of faith, with my pockets at a disadvantage, asked God if during the locked down (COVID-19 era), was the right time to begin matriculation of a doctoral degree? And just like God does for any of his children to which Balaam and Job agree, "*God is not like man*" and in Numbers 23:19. Some answers lingering, and others answered swiftly. Armed with confidence I moved forward in faith and trusting each step of the process while God supplied the grace, and favor that I needed to be successful.

The leadership theory for this era is servant leadership and most believe that they are servant leaders. However, I acknowledge now at the writing of this book that still I am unclear how to become a servant leader, or what servant leadership meant, but continued, trusting that after much prayer and preparation it would become transparent and clearer.

My father was employed as a caretaker on a small cay, and my mom was employed as a housekeeper. The environment dictated that they catered to the needs of the visitors and owners of the cay. As a result, these practices were engrained in me and my brother and as time went on, we became servants of others. Employment, as it is, is performed at the will of the employer. However, being a servant leader does not require us to serve our leaders or employers instead those who are in the trenches with us, often referred to as followers. Neither is serving dependent on conditions or circumstance. Most people would continue with caution as they approach a new idea or venture, but I did not, I went full steam ahead.

According to my parents, my entry into the world was a display of what my future would like, filled with fortitude, and willingness. After, praying for a daughter having had a miscarriage, I was born. I was born in the middle of tropical storm weather, on the island in the Bahamas called Lil Whale Cay in the Berry Islands. It was after dark because during that time light was only used in extreme emergencies, due to the use of generators. Luckily, there was a lady resident on the island who practiced midwifery that helped my birth. There was no doctor, no after delivery hospital stay, and I was not taken to see a doctor until two weeks after my birth. Imagine the trauma for my mother, only nineteen years old at the time. I was told that the storm was a notable display of my entrance, eyes opened at once, surveying the room as if it was a part of my role to ensure the safety and security of all present.

Can you imagine, I was Moses incarnate or what Moses felt like when he discovered that though he was secure in Pharaoh's kingdom, his assignment and purpose on earth was much larger than where he was placed at the time. Therefore, he did not take for granted the comforts provided in his current conditions. See Exodus 2: 11-12, Moses' heart towards his people could not be controlled when he saw the plight they endured. He killed an Egyptian and had to escape because he thought that after his deeds were revealed he would be killed by Pharaoh. It is a clear example that our purpose in life is not defined by us, and although we make plans and strategize, the results reveal that it is not our power control. Sadly, we discover sooner rather than later that the creator of humanity controls everything concerning us. Stated in Genesis 1:27 *"So God created humankind in his own image, in the image of God he created them; male and female he created them,"* which suggests that the authority belongs to God.

My family is of Caribbean origin, and although from different countries, there are duplicitous traits, and cultural practices. Therefore, our family gatherings consist of similar dishes, and activities. It is a common theme to have grits and some types of seafood like conch (shellfish), jack and grouper fish, or lobster at every family cooking experience. We practiced in most instances the same religion Baptist and Pentecostal, and our emotions were always high when it came to the wellbeing or correcting of family. The acronym I give to the word family is: **False Allies Made in Life Yearly**. They are supposed to be our vilest defenders and allies not our enemies, yet oppression and offense are suffered by their hands and mouths constantly. Family is where you learn how to socialize and share all your ideas, especially if your household was limited to sibling count. Nevertheless, I enjoyed family gatherings there we ate, gossiped, prayed, preyed, and counseled. Unfortunately, there are no anecdotes for families except God, the Creator.

I was and still am a religious individual who has since learned the difference between being religious and being spiritual. I enjoy being serenaded by gospel spirituals supplying an outlet and moments of escape. As you dig deeper into my life you will see that I was never without God. I was christened as a child in the Lutheran ministry, groomed Pentecostal in the Church of God Bahamas, Inc; married Baptist, baptized Church of God of Prophecy; married for the second time Episcopalian and married the third time into Church of God in the Bahamas. According to the self-righteous judgmental church goer, I am a serial fornicator.

The Right to Dream

I remain a dreamer, however, and I have the right to dream. My dream was and still is to live a happy peaceful life with all; to be rich, fierce, intellectual, and godly. I even imagine me being so kind that even my enemies would forget we are enemies (dreaming). However, I learned as I grew older that all things are for a season. I became clearer and more confident in my choices, and my character strengthened because of it. Dreaming allowed me the ability to reclaim my worth despite the abuses and traumas that I faced. For a moment visualize what it means to be fault free, and innocent according to Jude 1:24 *"Now all glory to God, who is able to keep you from falling away and will bring you with great joy into his glorious presence without a single fault"*. That would mean that you are perfectly imperfect and totally and completely blameless; and as a human I learned over the years that it is simply impossible.

Being faultless occurs nowhere in the history of humanity except where Jesus Christ is concerned. Even then for humankind to understand what it means to be genuinely human, God allowed Jesus to be born through a virgin named Mary to refute all future claims. Conceptually we are designed to conform to the internal environments of nature while the external environments are dictated by man, which poses many challenges to our existence. This concept reinforces that as humans, we are not participators in creation, but we stand outside of it while trying to influence what is designed already for its purpose and cannot be adjusted by us.

I will not LIVE in my past, but my past does have a role in my future. On April 1, 1989, as a bride my father walked me down the aisle in a lovely white dress, to songs that I chose with husband number one (yes you read right) – Evan. At the time it was the wedding of the year, in a small settlement called the Bight, Providenciales, in Turks and Caicos Islands. Like every young woman, being married is a part of that dream of a family, a husband who was religious, sanctified and Holy Ghost filled. The husband's attributes were to also include being a great father, an excellent communicator and lover. As I said, it was all a dream, in my active participation and imagination. In fact, my advice to the brides of the future is never become so desperate to change your name that you are blinded by the ceremony that lasts less than thirty minutes that you do not focus on the marriage. Be aware of what is acceptable in the institution of marriage, as it lends only to conformity of the other not the people who committed to it. What I have come to understand is, *"without knowledge. People perish"* I became a victim, an observer, and an explorer of that framework. I trusted everyone outside of the Inventor and Creator himself, and I paid heavily. Perceptively institutions in my view were made to be conformed to, not changed to suit our emotions.

However, not all the blame for the deterioration of marriage can or is extended to any of them be it Husband 1, and 2. I am extremely strong in nature as an individual. In earnest and honest critique, I am SO independent till I can become impatient if the other sex does not move at the speed of lightning as I imagine.

The example of marriage set by my parents who married the year I was born was imperfect; they lived separately from the time I was about nine years old. My father abused alcohol which made him aggressive towards my mother, which sometimes resulted in her being unable to care for herself and us for weeks, sometimes months. My father loved us, but his method of love was translated as supplying a roof over our heads, and his last name. Unfortunately, both of my parents had no examples to follow as their parents faced similar challenges.

Protection in marriage the way I envisioned was a myth, unavailable, advice was scarce and examples to imitate were few. As a couple our knowledge of God's word was novice, and our prayer life was non-existent. It was much easier to follow the model that was on television. Word of advice, that is an act called "Lights, Camera, Action." A terrible road map, where the lessons are still in the crack and the conclusion is highlighted as the only solution to the problem. The models from my grandparents suggested that tenure is better. Their examples had holes filled with secrets, silence, and sayings not a roadmap or avenue that would sustain my personal plans and goals. So, when the fire became hotter than hot, in disobedience and counsel I bowed out gracefully as I had seen too many dysfunctional relationships in my family. I was suffocating and moving forward was my only choice.

Moving Forward

To me, moving forward was not just a choice, but a motivation to succeed in life and legacy. Legacy demands that you exhaust all your efforts with the hope that the more positive ones will be cherished. Otherwise, what is the purpose of not ensuring that your imprint is left in the annals of your own heritage? Being born into a family supplies some footage but not all; it requires some of your own input, and desires to progress. No one can illustrate your values; values shape culture, and culture highlights your strengths as an individual. So, continue to dream.

There were many influences of a negative connotation that could ruin my future and constantly reminded me of my past. In the ninth grade, I experienced an injury from a motorbike during the Easter break from school on the island of Bimini. My mom periodically sent my brother and me to her sister in Bimini, or our grandparents in Grand Bahama, every break we had from school. The incident happened while trying to learn to ride a motorbike, which every child in Bimini knew how to do, if they could steer and keep the bike upright. My turn came and I did extremely well, except when getting off the bike to give someone else a turn. I burnt my leg on the muffler and did not seek medical help at once, resulting in a terrible infection that caused me to miss school the rest of the year, due to mobility issues. It turned out that was also an answer to my mom's prayer because she could not afford the balance of my school fees at Saint Augustine's College, Nassau Bahamas and I would have had to stay home anyway.

The quality of my life was threatened, my future stood in limbo, and in most instances, I felt as if I was all alone.

Abuse was a member of the family

Familial ties defined by me stand for your connection to others, or your acquaintance with a thing. Membership supplies the opportunity for an association to be formed and a connection to be set up based on familiarity. I came from a foundation that was built on prayer and praise, but in this segment, I needed protection and power. The building had cracks and the seams were beginning to become more visible to the exterior. My parents did the best they could, but sometimes their best involved digging deeper, longer, and being consistent in reinforcements.

It was before puberty, and menstrual cycle in 1977, that sexual abuse and incest started for me, a young girl. No prayer in my recollection stopped that or prevented the first incident and others from following. The violations lasted from 11 – 14 years old. As I now reflect, I had knowledge of this act among family members, but no one seemed to cry out for help. In hindsight, we thought it was normal. Victims of sexual abuse are not as vocal, due to fear, and stigma while wishing the attention that they look for without having to request it themselves. Consequently, alluding to frivolous excuses and using the opportunity to raise awareness of their own abuse as their reasons for hurting others.

I was innocent but because I was advanced in intellect and innocently friendly, it was interpreted as my being "fast," "swift," "rude." My options were limited, and support was unavailable." No justice, No Peace"! I am not sure if that is authored by anyone, but I heard it said in various demonstrations for causes whether for salary negotiations or civil injustice to humanity. Never mind my innocence being exploited; the perpetrators were never punished, and even now I cast blame on myself and have lived a life of trauma and shame in my head for a long time. I have come to realize that events were designed to break me but, I WON. For many years after and during I cried and was disappointed that adults who were aware of similar instances happening to others closely related often referred to it as a joke and encouraged shame to silence them, and pride to corrupt them until recently.

The support system was weak, my parents were not present in mindset or listening, as they were too busy surviving and defending themselves in other matters. The traumas of sexual abuse propelled me to find solace in the arms of abusers as an adult. Eventually as a youth activity that did not involve being around my abusers, often spending the weekend with friends that I met at church. Often drowning my sorrows in books was a favorite pastime that kept me dreaming and hoping, even singing which is another favorite pastime. I learned early who the "vilest defender" of me was. It was God and He kept me. Abuse of any kind disrupts peace. Peace is the key to unlocking potential and opportunities in one's life.

Gaining My Voice

My belief is that self-representation comes natural to all human beings. It is an empowerment that strives to confirm who we are at contrasting times. According to my mother, I was not shy in my childhood, more specifically during my elementary years she recalls outbursts or times when I did a decent job of standing for myself. A proud moment for her was my elementary years and my ability to excel academically, and my tenure in politics was birth. I was getting good grades, over talking, and ensuring everyone knew my name. I started with Ms. Estelle's School through Washington Street in Nassau Bahamas. Bright and eager, always the leader, taking part, volunteering, and leading whatever activity I was involved in. School plays, team competitions, and some sports more like cheerleading. I am not an athlete.

In my transition to grade school, my mom said I continued without any breaks. My formative years saw me taking part in choir. I and those around me began to recognize my highly opinionated voice, resulting in roles such as one of the team members of Palmdale Primary School's team in which I took part in a program called "It's Academic" that came on ZNS TV station in the Bahamas in the late seventies. This program covered English, Math, Social Studies, and World Affairs, and I was honored even then to be apart. Although successful, as a child and eventually as an adult, I adopted many fables that had to be unraveled, erased, and unlearned through my adolescent to adult stage. One such fable was that women are to be seen and not heard. Women in my family were and are still strong but remain passive. I am certain that the author's intent of this known cliché had its purpose, except I grew up in the early seventies when young black girls were involuntary participants of women's rights as dictated by the current times and season.

The ability to receive an elementary education, something my father was unable to do, and my mom a limited amount because she was the oldest girl and had to help her mom with chores and children, was priceless. I earned my voice, my place, and became self-aware of competition, recognizing that it was a form of growth. Meanwhile these new revelations were times of enlightenment since my focus was centered on the ability to communicate and respond in the environment.

Period of Uncertainty

Innocently, most people can identify as either cold, hot, or lukewarm in their emotions, while enforcing boundaries in areas of frustration and social enjoyment. My involvements in social activities were my refuge from a dysfunctional home and abuse. My mom ensured that I socialize with other girls because my only biological sibling was a boy. I imagine since she was the second born of her siblings, she knew well that the stimulations girls need with the same sex are not offered in the opposite sex. The importance of having a girlfriend who is like a sister is priceless to a girl with no sisters. Grant it, as things change, and life goes on, even those connections can prove fatal in the long term.

My childhood best friend, Araline was meticulous, mindful, and a muscle, my muscle. No one could touch me when she was around, and I mean no one. To date, almost forty-five years later her daughter, Candace who I claim as my niece, is often heard saying to either of us, "I am not getting in mommy and your business." My female best friend had sisters and yet she chose to include me in their family. Whenever I was in her presence I felt a sense of security, and the wisdom that she imparted caused me to be relieved from many hardships that were known to me. The book of Ecclesiastes 4: 9 (MSG) confirms: "*It's better to have a partner than go it alone*". I did not always listen to all her advice and sometimes found myself in situations and relationships that caused me to experience much pain.

In fact, from a child people were jealous of me and I could not understand as I did not have much. I was poor. However, what I later realized is that they recognized the power of my potential. I did not know it then, but I do know this relationship was key to my future, as uncertainty lurked. The oppression was real in the era that included my teens, the unraveling of who I was to become was being peeled. Uncertainty challenged my seasons. The scope of who I was to become had begun to be unfolded. There are so many reasons to not want to be a part of such changes, yet if our desire is to be transformed, it is unavoidable and each of us has a role to play, and we must show up.

In fact, some of us believe and practice our daily lives in hopes of having others save us from ourselves. What I have come to figure out is, life is a bunch of circumstances not predicated on what we think, or feel, as the battle rages within us, and humanity responds. Humanity expects approval and acceptance as standards of care, yet the fear of embracing these elements prevents us from moving forward or expressing our true sentiments. Our desire implies the perpetrator is external, and we are justified in our will to remain.

Not dealing with any issue in life in totality prevents us from moving forward and blocks the ability to achieve authentically. Restrictions in any form are an objection to the criterion of the quality of life we should keep. Quality of life insinuates the exercise of committing and responding in wisdom to the portions of discomfort in your journey that may arise. Each setback, whether personal or professional, in nature is a constant reminder of how disruptive and unsettling it is, erasing what is possible and attainable in life for all individuals.

David wrote in Psalms 37:23 (NLT), "*The Lord directs the steps of the godly. He delights in every detail of their lives*" no wonder I am a warrior, I was determined and have decided not to allow any of my challenges to cause me to miss what God had in store me. The dream of home ownership as immigrants did not happen for my parents; fear crippled them. False and misleading information caused missed opportunities. Even though my father shared interests in a farm that I later learned was on someone else's land, he still used it at a level subpar to his potential. The connections in business crippled his efforts to obtain and reach further self-employment and, at death, the best tenant to his landlord for 26 years, no repairs or maintenance ever asked, and the rent was never late.

No photographic lens can adequately capture the imprint of experience that life offers. In this regard our journeys are picturesque and complete with examples often laced with pain. Pain produces energy; ask the mothers of every species that walks or roams this earth. Pain is flawless; it has after its own kind (meaning that pain can only be pain) and is not answerable to any. The outcomes of pain are clear on the delivery of the result. In this instance a leader is challenged, and one's ability to lead flawlessly. Such inflictions cumulatively include our response: NO FAULT.

Nurture

"The root your hand has planted, the son you have raised up

for yourself," Psalms 80:15

People often mistake nurturing as a sudden claim to fame which usually comes in legacy, heritage, or money, and most often from the first two of the three as for the last, you either must be born into it or fall into it by chance when placing anywhere between one in one hundred million – the lottery. The same can be said about our genealogy: who we are or propose to be to the end is from the beginning submerged in our lineage. My parents were born in two Caribbean countries, Haiti and Turks and Caicos Islands; though close in proximity vastly different in culture, and landmass. My parents had two children in their marriage, my brother, now deceased to whom they gave the name Jeffery Lincoln Emmanuel, and me. We were born in the Commonwealth of the Bahamas in 1967 and 1968, respectively.

My dad, born in Haiti, according to my grandfather (Claudius Emmanuel) was kidnapped by him as a sailor to that country in the late 1950's. The Republic of Haiti's story is still popular from the revolution with British and French colonizers in the late 1700's and early 1800's. Haiti is commonly referred to as the wealthiest and poorest country in the Americas, specifically, the Caribbean basin of Islands. Rich because they have since stood against the tentacles slavery and race, and as a result, continuously suffer and need of systemic and standardized functional infrastructure that will hopefully supply economic gains and Inland Revenue to sustain the growth and development of their country. The lack encourages the migration of the citizens of Haiti on treacherous waters, in unsafe crafts to other countries which causes public health concerns and the elasticizing of primary health budgets.

The Turks and Caicos Islands is recorded to have a population of around forty-two thousand persons, although it feels like an estimated sixty thousand. Turks and Caicos Islands are a beautiful archipelago of islands southeast of the Bahamas Islands and the envy of its tourism sister and brother countries surrounding her. Commonly referred to as TCI, it is one of those countries that see an influx of Haitian migrants on an average of 300 per month. The arrival of migrants causes exorbitant costs to governments that involve staff, shelter, medical attention, food, and repatriation. There are no minerals for extraction in this country. The exportation of conch and lobster orchestrated by seasons are the only two that generate external incomes indirectly for the government. Tourism dominates revenue generation, with constant prayers that there is no hurricane- productions annually that could leave the country halted in tourism visitation and imports due to weather conditions and damages to homes, buildings, and ports for weeks.

My mother was born in the late 1940's and given the name Vanis Rosealee. A citizen of Turks and Caicos Islands, she grew up with her parents who later migrated to the Bahamas; my father – Christie Levi (he gave himself a second name) did as well with his family. My mother is the second born of twelve siblings while my father, who did not meet his biological family until adulthood is the oldest in his adopted family. Both parents were psychologically traumatized by life events before becoming adults. As a young black Caribbean woman, from a low class and low-income household living from paycheck to paycheck, and immigrant parents' where the norm meant functioning in silence for fear of being found out. Making being heard not only essential, but vital. On many occasions the injustices were reason enough, but we chose not to complain although we (my brother and I) were suffering.

The traumas of my parents trickled to me and my brother as we often experienced mental health issues at tender ages caused by alcoholism, physical abuse and verbal abuse at the hands of them and others. These experiences breathe life into the cliche "that you are what you eat." They were victims, my brother and I were victims, and our children became victims, hereditary in nature.

Identity

It is my belief that leaders are born and made. My mother was in practice her entire life, and even at this stage of her life with early dementia she continues to work on her lucid days as though she is in charge. In one of her stories telling moments which come often, my mother at the age of 12 years old, was denied the right to further her education because she had to help her mother in the care of her younger siblings. Colorful were those days for her yet she chooses even today to view them as here best days, symbolic of a person who enjoyed meeting the needs of others. The loss of childhood allowed my mom to learn life skills early in life and earned the title of decision maker due to the absence of her immigrant working-class surviving parents.

My mother was sharp, and a thriving woman despite many adversities faced, through real life experience. In our communities we labeled these kind of people as "street smart", learning as they go to speak and perform. Mommy earned positions made up of being a community and nation builder. As an employee she was shop-steward (union representative) in the hotel union, on her job at Club Med Bahamas, elevating from being a beadsman (beads were the hotel currency, no cash or other form of payment was accepted) to a supervisor, matron in a lodge called the Eastern Stars, Supervisor - laundry, at Grace Bay Club, and Chaplain of the People's Democratic Movement in the Turks and Caicos Islands BWI. I am not the daughter of slothful, lazy, unambitious parents. My mom was a leader in all aspects, and she took her roles seriously, especially where people were involved. The joy of advocating and helping people become the better version of them was empowerment to her.

On the other hand, my father thrived in leadership as a male thriving due to the hand he was dealt in life. Being so far away from his biological parents, he yearned to be able to afford to care for them even at a distance, trying many entrepreneurial endeavors to sustain himself and support them once he learned of their existence. Although a functioning alcoholic who physically abused his wife through extramarital affairs, producing five other children, he loved to work and work he did while embracing opportunities to socialize while enlarging his family. I met three of my siblings from my father at his death which has been recorded in his Bible. Well, I can only say I know them by name and birth dates. He was persistent in encouraging my brother and me to get an education or good jobs. My Dad loved farming and our time with him was consistent with weekend visits to a farm of which he was part–owner. Oh, I hated this, but it was his way of displaying his love, I guess. We were never told that he was part–owner until we were adults.

My father in life was known to be an abuser, and one time during an incident between my mom and him, he shoved in the oven by him leaving her incapable of caring for herself or us for months. He assumed she was a turkey, so he baked her. The scar is still there today. Unfortunately, after most acts of this type of behavior my mom took him back after many tears and apologies, only to be repeated at least every instance he got drunk, came home with no money, and got upset that my mom was unable to fill the gap financially. Until my mom left my dad, she was able to keep a job. Even though he did not attend church regularly he was highly religious and often chided that if he attended church he wanted only one role, to collect the offering.

Foundation

"Does a farmer always plow and never sow? Is he forever cultivating the soil and never planting?" Isaiah 28:24 (NLT)

Before I became reality, I was a thought, so says Jeremiah 1:5. "B*efore I shaped you in the womb, I knew all about you*". My mom had 2 pregnancies before me, and one after my brother who survived. My father was physically abusive, and my mother was too young, impressionable, and desperate for ways out of poverty to defend herself. Meanwhile, my background in business, politics and religion was founded on principles that dictated form, fashion, and show. Many times, I was forced to be something other than myself to ensure that the group looked good.

I faced instances where I hardly recognized how important a foundation was in who you are, and who you were to become in life, and to my future. One of the times I speak about is traveling to the Turks and Caicos for the first time in 1982 on a cargo plane, sitting in a chair made for a dining room. We often take for granted in bigger countries the hardships experienced by others in Third World countries for their daily survival. Ed Haggier (name change due to copyright infringement), the pilot during that time as a favor of my grandmother's employer, Babbie Earlson transported my brother and me on summer vacation from the Bahamas to the Turks and Caicos Islands, giving my mom a much-needed break as all her family had moved back to the TCI.

The plane landed safely on Providenciales, and we were greeted by a customs officer in a small, tiny building, which seemed odd as the building we left out of in Nassau was much larger and more customer friendly than this one. After being released to leave the airport, my brother and I later learned that our transportation to my grandmother's house had to be booked in advance since there was only one vehicle on Providenciales at the time, which meant we would have to spend the night at a cousin's home in a parish called Five Cays which was closer to the airport. Family is important to me, but what amazed me most was the love, patience, and unity that dwelled among them, even in distance did not deteriorate their attention to the needs of each other. The surprise was the mode of transport to get to our cousin's house, a donkey. This left me and my brother speechless. Immediately I began to voice my opinionated comment and the pilot and customs officer thought it was so hilarious, they laughed.

The Bahamas at the time was a more developed country. Our father had a car even though we only rode in it on weekend trips to the farm, and there was a bus service. This trip was slated to be fun, but already disappointments kept being added, and from a distance, my brother and I could see the donkey and the owner drawing nearer to the airport. As immigrants in the Bahamas, my parents were discriminated against, and received terroristic threats that caused them to live in fear. I also remember that as a child my maternal grandmother left the Bahamas in 1974 to return to her country, but my grandfather did not go, so I assumed that we were all Bahamians. Now arriving here to visit them, aligned all our imaginative thoughts, all they had was a donkey to transport us to a place to stay for the night, 'they must have been out of their minds' I thought. Thankfully, I saw a truck coming in the distance headed in the small airport terminal direction saving the day. There would be no donkey ride for us. Oh boy! I was relieved.

I never had that experience ever again. We arrived safely at Kingstown in Providenciales of the Turks and Caicos Islands, covered in white quarry from the road that we travelled as passengers on the back of the truck. The roads were unpaved, and the truth is there were no designated roads, as at the time development was extremely low. Yet the adventure ushered us into another reality we did not prepare for. We came face to face with the genealogical foundation that belonged to our mother; and the only reality that my father acknowledged as home at the time. There was no running water through faucets or by pump, no electricity, no streetlights, and no indoor toilets, in fact. We spent the best eight weeks there without complaints and did not die. We fondly remember it as some of the best days of our childhood.

Legacy

Legacy is important, and it illustrates what we value, and our response to it. Our descendants will reflect and reminisce on our steps and our stops. There will be questions, and insights into the choices we selected. Our mission and goals must be clear. We were Turks and Caicos Islanders, at least according to the law at the time by extension British Citizens. The importance of legacy is found by the foundation. In hindsight when in the Bahamas the distinctiveness of who we were stood out, because of style, culture and practice. Our work ethic was different – not because of migration. Our styles are still superior and bourgeois, and our culture is filled with arousing aromas that are second to none. Such revelation makes me realize the gravity without prejudice and fear that my presence on the earth was designed from start to completion. I was born to die, and die I did in many instances.

My life adventures were filled with strong, weak, challenged, growth and development moments, but so is my present and my future will, also. In one of my daily times with God, in 1999 in the USA from a program called "Life in the Word", I gleaned the importance of how to ensure that my future according to God's word included my participation, as cited in Luke 18:8. Empowered with this knowledge, on October 22, 1999, I acted, by doing the following: staying aware, trusting God in the process, motivating myself, engaging, competing, and being patient. I was facing my future, and unseating fear. My record of success was limited with a line of passive women, abusive men, and the list continues.

As an Alum of Palmdale Primary, Saint Augustine's College, and the famous 'Pacer Nation' – R. M. Bailey High school, I graduated from high school in 1985. I had a foundation in education that is second to none, from elementary to tertiary level. I was shaped, molded, and set up. My favorite teachers were Mrs.

Hepburn Miller, Beaut Moss, Mrs., Richardson, and Ms. Francis, Charles Mackey, and Mr. Horn. At Palmdale Primary I was groomed as praise and worship leader, and I learned the confidence of expressing myself. At Saint Augustine's I had my first experience with Catholicism, where chapel was mandatory every Wednesday, and in English language class, Mrs. Richardson was sure to correct my grammar and phonics attempts. As an R.M. Bailey Pacer, I returned to my roots; the school's patron was married to a Turks and Caicos Islander formerly Adams. Here my love for math was formulated. I had my first taste of alcohol. I learned to skip classes, and I did not receive a diploma at graduation but rather a high school leaving certificate – with a 1.88 GPA.

Boastfully my children, Cobreti, Eurydice, and Linquet are all college graduates, Claudius (beginning sophomore year as this book is written), a proud member of his university band a drum major, make me immensely proud of their accomplishments. My hunger to thrive, and leave my mark on the earth has empowered me to contrive the following framework in the legacy:

Trust (Future Oriented) PLANS

Share time PERSPECTIVES

Characterize my GOALS

Align the CULTURE

Monitor my SUCCESSES

Sacrifice my DESIRES

Establish my VALUES

We can prosper in all things if we do the work, but doing the work is only half of success. The other half is ensuring that others who are willing receive the level of mentoring and coaching necessary for them to achieve also. Model, model, and turn the dialogue into examples they must look at after your demise. Financial Planning is one such example, as you know even in the Caribbean; we must pool funds to bury the dead. I was introduced to financial planning in 1999 at Best Elementary School, during a parent meeting for my daughter Eurydice. At that meeting, a financial advisor was in attendance and offered opportunities to parents to start securing their future for their children.

While some of the suggested limits were small, since that meeting I have held variable life insurance that supplies loans to the insured on the term of the insurance. I experienced car trouble one Christmas and had no money to finance the repairs. Guess who I borrowed that money from to have the repairs done, myself. It has proven beneficial to my financial portfolio in times of economic hardship. Since then, I have increased my portfolio to include mutual funds and stock options. My generations will know because not only will I teach them, but I will model for them as well.

Financial literacy is vital to the financial growth of people with all levels of incomes. Sadly, though these programs are currently more accessible the rise of inflation has caused those communities to remain stagnant. Ceremoniously in the religious culture we were always encouraged to tithe, and sow a seed, but the practicality of these scriptures inadequately explained. Ultimately resulting in more responsibility on the church treasury to support and sustain the lifestyle of its members.

Culturally our village thrived on asue's. Asue is a money saving system where a group of people pool their funds for a set time and at the date decided by them, they would get their draw (amount of funds they give) held by one person during the length of the exercise. Asue is a very risky system with no insurance or procedure in the event of loss (theft) or death. Normally this would last for a year, sometimes twice a year. Most people of color in the Caribbean prefer this system to banks, and prefer the risk associated to save monies for building their homes, sending their kids to college, and a vacation. Suggestion: this is a risk, investing in a safer method such as a banking system that works the same and is more secure.

OPPORTUNITIES

"We are hard-pressed on every side, yet not crushed; we are perplexed, but not in despair; persecuted, but not forsaken; struck down, but not destroyed." 2 Corinthians 4: 8-9

Opportunities are two-sided; they propel and extract your goals and plans. On one side we are challenged to overcome the obstacles, so that we may meet opportunities. Obstacles can also infuse motivation to research thoroughly and persuade to act.

In these seasons I experienced homelessness, fired as an employee, discriminated against, and treated as a child because one of my parents thought that I should stop dreaming. I experienced almost dropping out of school, my children bullied, culture shock, and learning to drive on six lane highways. The seasons changed in Houston. We had cold temperatures that were beyond what we were accustomed in tropical Turks and Caicos Islands. My son, in his desire to be friendly with others faced drug addiction, and abuse.

The obstacles were many as I rose through the ranks. I was a single parent and I paid for my own education. Employers did not recognize my qualifications. I was intimidated by the culture, and the environment. My parents always believed that I should be working in an office as a clerk or secretary, never the manager or owner of a joint. I moved through the ranks as a temporary telephone operator position at Club Med (Bahamas & Turks and Caicos Islands) in 1987- 88. Once that assignment was complete, I moved on to an unfamiliar path of becoming an Immigration officer (6 months), meter reader at Provo Power Company (1st woman meter reader, 1st woman electronics engineer in Turks and Caicos Islands), proceeded by positions as Office Manager at Coral Construction, Engineers Assistant with Cable and Wireless, Ltd, and return to Meter Reader at Provo Power Company. While all these jobs were in the technical field, I noticed none were fulfilling, but I kept telling myself all I needed was a foot in the door, and then something would happen to me. Foot in the door theory, however, never worked for me.

Likewise, if you do not sell yourself, no one will do it moderately or adequately for you or on your behalf. There was no support for me as a qualified woman in technology and engineering with an Associates of Science Electronics Engineering Degree with Biomedical specialty. In the Turks and Caicos there is an Honors Awards (2016) initiative that recognizes the outstanding contributions of the citizens. I was not recognized at the inaugural or continuing events because I kept my mouth shut. Instead, historically another young lady worthy of honor also, received the award as the country's first woman engineer (youth). Did people remember my contribution? Quite possibly? Did they sound my horn? Absolutely not! I came to the field during a heavy infiltration of male dominance, and I obtained the same or even more qualifications than they did. The tolerance for my sex was low, so while my supervisors and fans were impressed, I was not allowed to prove my skills or training in areas other than meter reading or be celebrated for my academic achievements.

As of today, I am a well-oiled machine as it pertains to academia; in tribute to my father, his words, and no offense to anyone, I am too "Edumacated" for my own good!

Academia

Education was a core value at home, yet I failed high school. My parents were average parents making promises, and boasting about their children to their friends, but their investment was minimal as all they could afford was my uniform and my lunch. At the time they did the best that they could, and I took and passed the entrance exams paid for by my godmother in May 1979 to attend Saint Augustine's College, a prestigious catholic high school, and a dream. They had good intentions for three years, but my mom constantly remained in debt alone to pay my school fees, which saw my dream come down as shattering glass. I had to be transferred to the R.M. Bailey Senior High School in Nassau, Bahamas where I completed high school in 1985 with a school leaving certificate. To me, where was the loyalty in that? My dad was the culprit in this issue. Excelling in achievements, whether academic, work, or community, sometimes for a moment, removes the pain of what you are dealing with now or at a time. For me, achievement became an outlet to exhale and transform into something and someone else. I used education as my outlet, omitting the pain of the process while persevering in the journey. Honestly, I believed then and stood on the scripture in Psalms 127 verse 1 ~ *"Unless the Lord builds the house, the builders' labor in vain...."*

In September 1997, I enrolled in the Industrial Training Center to pursue a vocational study in Electrical Installation. The highlight of my life was I always tried to partake in non-traditional pursuits as a young woman. However, due to my being late in registration because of the death and funeral of my grandfather (Robert C. Hutcherson, RIP, 1997), the only available program that had vacant seats were the night class, so I embraced the opportunity. The goal was to obtain some technical licensure to secure a job at Bahamas Electrical Corporation in the Bahamas, or then, Provo Power Company in Turks and Caicos Islands.

Technical qualifications are good, but it was not my goal. Finally, after many attempts and applications for financial aid to complete tertiary level studies I was awarded a scholarship to study, and like lightning after one year the scholarship was taken away. I felt cheated but I was determined to complete what God had made possible for me without the help of those I perceived had my back.

The exercise of pivoting from a life of poverty to a promise of more meant going the extra mile, and education mattered. I matriculated at the University of Houston – Victoria, achieving a Bachelor of Applied Arts & Science Degree in Business and Leadership, followed by a Master of Arts Interdisciplinary Studies – Leadership and Nonprofit Management. I had the ability, and was willing, and God supplied the resources in 2005 and 2008.

The dream of receiving higher education was always a present thought in my mind except I always wanted a Doctoral degree. No, I did not want to be a Doctor of Medicine, just a doctor. Let me tell you when God has something purposed for your life, it will happen whether you are in full participation or not. I took the next step and like the commercial, "*Take the Next Step, apply today and receive a scholarship for $250 towards your next class*", I began taking classes. For me, another act in my life to prove to those still pondering if God is alive, He is. Faith gives no thought for tomorrow because tomorrow takes care of itself, and with that I applied and got accepted into the Doctoral Strategic Leadership – Servant Leadership program at Regent University, and at the writing of this book will graduate soon.

Me Too

"Heaviness in the heart of man maketh it stoops:

But a good word maketh it glad," Proverbs

12:25 (NLT)

Overcoming in life is complex and not fancy. It demands commitment and dedication. Psalms 127: 3 states that "...*children are a heritage of the LORD: And the fruit of the womb is his reward*". This I believe is not directed at parents only, but to deceiving adults. Regardless of whether there is evidence that they know or are exposed, for the benefit of children these perpetrators should be lynched when discovered, and not given a right to a defense.

Eventually, I ended up being raised in a single-parent home as my mother could no longer endure physical abuse from my father. In fact, from the age of nine until I was fourteen, I suffered sexual abuse or RAPE, by men whom my mother called brothers and boyfriends. Did I report them? I tried. The cycle prevented my voice, and my pain, from being heard. What was more alarming was that my mother herself, in her past being denied childhood, was not sensitive to my plight and was never a good listener (dementia lurked before now). She dismissed whatever my concerns were, especially if they were outside the parameters of food, clothes, or school supplies. I was fondled, groped, and penetrated all with my eyes shut tight, hoping and praying for the act to be over, and for it to stop. These acts were so invasive until I began to believe that they were acceptable to a girl child, and that this was how womanhood was to be introduced.

My parents trusted my brother and me with individuals at face value who saw us as fresh meat, vulnerable, innocent, and naïve. WE often presented our case only to be sent on vacations or left alone with certain people, to endure more abuse. The violations lasted approximately five years, but the trauma has remained throughout my life. I was robbed of my puberty and accepted that the responsibility was mine to protect myself, not vice versa. My brother and I were left to defend ourselves. On his deathbed (March 12, 1993), he made me promise to take care of his daughter –, as he did not want her to fall prey to the hands of evil people who would choose to slaughter her future for their selfish gain. Unfortunately, I was only given a partial opportunity at 16 years old.

Such traumas are significant to one's mental health, a danger to the orientation of each sex and sexual response. It can also be associated with a cry for help when you find a compatible mate from God, and a cause for concern. Dating for me was hard; the one person that I believed was for me walked away from me because I was damaged goods. For many years after my first marriage, I refused to accept that I was worthy of someone's love and care and chose to have occasional meetups. Meetups are dangerous to the soul, body, and mind, because you end up giving a prize that is extremely significant in marriage, and family away. The memories of not being able to fully focus and concentrate on puberty, grades, and fashion as a teenager overwhelmed me. Many days my value was worthless, and until I read somewhere, "that I was a seed." The thought resonated with me and helped me to keep standing up, but Jeremiah 29:11 moved the goal stick in my life, activating purpose and the formulation of plans; "*For I know my plans for you, declares the Lord, "plans' to prosper you and not to harm you, plans to give you hope and a future".*

Fortunately, my brother and I also had some good people in our lives who at various times supported my mother, and encouraged the involvement of religion, causing me to hear God's promises repeated often, for example in Girls Brigade:

Motto: "*Seek Serve and to follow Christ*".

Aim: "*To help girls to become followers of Jesus Christ, through self-control reverence and responsibility, to find true enrichment in life*"; and,

The principles: "Acknowledges *Jesus Christ as Savior and Lord according to the Scriptures and seeks to fulfil its aim to the Glory of One God, Father, Son and Holy Spirit Witnesses to the standard set by Jesus Christ and gives positive teaching on the*

Christian attitude to life promotes a just society where all people

are equally valued"

To me, religious programs at the time were more sincere or facilitators than the ones now.

Immigrants

> *"Hope deferred makes the heart sick, but a*
>
> *longing fulfilled is a tree of life," Proverbs*
>
> *13:12, NIV.*

The zodiac sign of a Gemini is twins; even though I do not subscribe to horoscopes, I was purposely born in this season and can be referred to as the comeback kid. In August 1999, a new landmass, culture, and people became our new home to – Cobreti and Eurydice and me. Recently divorced, I was awarded a partial scholarship to study at Houston Community College System – Electronics Engineering program, with no promise of employment. Thankfully, due to the generosity of a kind gentleman that I dated at that time, which I will call Ben, my children and I moved to America and one of my dreams became a reality.

I migrated to the United States of America on a student visa (F-1) with my children, it was not easy, but we survived. In true God fashion when we commit our plans to Him, He blesses. As a result, God placed us strategically in the paths and hands of his trusted caretakers, who supplied wisdom, support, and no judgment. The support system was immaculate, strong, and right, and only Romans 10:10 could adequately describe my sentiments, and I quote, *"For it is with your heart that you believe and are justified, and it is with your mouth that you profess your faith and are saved."* I was so excited about the opportunity and not a stranger to obstacles facing every door with optimism. Here I was in a strange land, the only person I could call on that would not judge me was my mother, and none of the people that were assigned to me was her.

Becoming an immigrant sometimes is all the choice that some people have, dating back to the historical book, the Bible. Jesus, Joseph, and Moses were examples in the Bible that one way or the other became immigrants not because of their own making, but they were forced to do so. Migration is not always ugly; it could be beautiful and when done right it can bloom like rose petals. The mix of culture and values that immigrants bring adds to the flavor of society and the mixture of differences.

June 2015, as I waited on the bench of the United States Embassy in the Bahamas, I was reminded of that day my mom came home with papers in her hand from a school in the United States in the state of Florida saying my brother and I were to attend. I was about eleven years old, and my brother was twelve. We were so excited, my brother and me. We shared the news with our friends and even had a going away party. Let me tell you the process was not completed. Never discuss your plans before you are sure that everything is in place. However, delay does not mean denial and my first migration happened when I was nineteen years old when I moved to the Turks and Caicos Islands. The interviewer asked personal questions like 'who had become a United States Citizen and sponsored me'? His final question was why do you want to migrate to the USA? My response in my head at first was, "I don't want to", but what came out of my mouth was, "it is the greatest country in the world, and the opportunities to grow are vast". With that, the loud thump of a stamp, and the words "Welcome to the United States", I became a legal permanent resident.

Based on the unlimited broadcasting of political and social opinions about migration, immigrants face the same social and emotional abuse whether in right standing and without regard for their country of origin. Such reactions cause one to ponder in thought if we are truly our brother's keeper? Most of us that migrated did so for the vastness of opportunity. Migration is a revolving door holding two faces: the face of the want, and the face of need. When in a place of power, the mighty must show the character and demeanor of the humble.

Sadly, we are all still challenged in how to achieve this, but I pray we get it sooner rather than later.

FOR

Before I formed you in the womb I knew you,

before you were born, I set you apart; I

appointed you as a prophet to the nations."

Jeremiah 1:5

Roadmaps, matrixes, project management templates are jargon and templates geared toward supplying focus and direction. Decision-making, awareness, analysis, and guidance are vital to setting up concrete relationships from becoming insolent. Meanwhile behaviors find priority to be a nuisance, and often seek ways out. In fact, being focused requires influence, strategy, planning, and foresight. In finding focus, the answer is already formulated especially since you were chosen before you were even created, and foundation formed according to Jeremiah 1:5. In every good thing planted, evil lurks and is waiting for any opportunity to rob you of that future and stopping at nothing to set up its prominence.

Fear Came First

The first year (1999) of migration to the United States of America was a daunting one. My eldest, Cobreti, was in middle school and from day one faced gang initiation, being robbed of his clothing, and being excluded by the minority races for being intellectually sound. For his survival he had to reduce his ability educationally, and become reincarnated to fit in. This was all new to my family since we came from a country where everyone was familiar with each other, and the participation in education is celebrated and encouraged. As a teenager he was traumatized slightly, before he embraced it as an opportunity to prove his leadership and independence.

In 2001, the queries shifted from middle school to high school. It was at Thurgood Marshall High School (Fort Bend ISD) that the Assistant Principal alerted me of an altercation involving some kids including my son. I had to leave my job which was forty-five minutes away with traffic flowing freely to collect from him from campus. Cobreti, I later learned, was cited for being in a fight with two other students. Immediately, I became frustrated, after receiving a citation that required him to attend court before his return to school.

The court date came, and I wished this were the only one, but I must acknowledge that this was one of many. After he got a driver's license, speeding tickets were his favorite. In the courtroom before our turn, I saw anxious and frustrated parents that felt like the system failed them and was only designed to familiarize their children with the judicial process from one side. There was no support for the theory that we as parents failed our children. Cobreti's turn before the judge was extremely hilarious. The opponents, looking to earn rites of passage into a gang, stood on the opposite side of him. They were 4 feet 9 inches tall, and my son at that time stood 6 feet 2 inches tall. For the twins to become a part of this gang, they had to pick a fight with my son and win. The picture of what it would look like came to the forefront of the audience in the entire court, and everyone burst into laughter when the judge examined and read the complaint provided by the school. The outcome of the trial was for Cobreti to receive behavioral counselling for 90 days (about 3 months).

Instead of allowing his parents to stand for him, Cobreti in many instances orchestrated his own defense and won. All my children are sufficiently capable of using words to defend themselves (hand over eyes) and they always did so confidently. The principal at the school was familiar with my number and called often just to inform me of his detentions, but often stopped short of praising his courageous response as I assumed that she wanted him to know that his actions had consequences. Despite his actions, however, there were also proud moments to be celebrated as well.

Another fearful moment was my departure from the USA after earning my bachelor's degree, and the fulfillment of a promise to my grandmother and bond signed with the Turks and Caicos Islands Government. Reluctantly, I returned to Turks and Caicos Islands, to supply financially for the cost of my children education, as they remained in the United States of America with no Pell grant aid or student loans. I was fearful because I had to rely on someone who had no formal experience of child rearing, much less teenagers, and an infant baby to stand in the gap, my second spouse - Dwayne. Nevertheless, he committed, focused, and did an excellent job and with the help of my mother those children are productive citizens in society.

My prayer and Bible study life increased as fear for my children's lives increased. They were developing from one stage of life to another. It was during this time that my son made me a grandmother, and the effects of cultural practices and changes at times became overwhelming. I met my girl, and my other daughter, and was stretched to the limit. The unimaginable happened during this season. She allowed me to love her, but soon after she left me one day, ill advised, but later returned with an apology, and I can still claim her.

I am a Caribbean girl, from a small island state where everyone knew everyone. The practice of trusting daily in God's guidance and the help of new friends with the social changes affected my family deeply. Let me tell you, it was only the beginning. The adversity I faced was great, and equally the stories; but the partnerships were outstanding. My mom became one of them and saw my battles and victories. I thank her for her prayers.

Organizations

Church was familiar to me, as my grandmothers were model prayer warriors, and consistent Sunday school attendees. The practice coupled with my own efforts and exposure as an adult to so many faith practices. In true human fashion, I strayed from what was foundational and proven effective, often reverting when demanding times hit. Thankfully, the move to Texas, and the southern Baptist experience, restored my prayer life and supported my dependence on God's amazing grace. This restoration occurred, often to the amazement of my friends, within a church membership of 98 percent Caucasian. To balance the minority in participation, I was often asked to take part in leadership roles from the Sunday school, Choir, and women groups. This was God is doing, and according to them during that time this was highly unlikely in Texas.

I felt that the fear of not winning was more of a motivation for me than being fearful. From 2009 – 2012 the Turks and Caicos Islands, my country, was under direct rule by the British Government. The Turks and Caicos Islands are still to this day an Overseas Territory of the United Kingdom, but my hope is to see an

80

independent nation before I am called home to be with the Lord. However, the political administration at that time was being prosecuted for unlawful acts as a person of public interest which resulted in the constitution of the country being suspended. The times were extremely uncertain to all citizens of the Turks and Caicos Islands and many of us were at risk of losing all that we had earnestly worked for.

After much consultation and much of the tax dollars spent on frivolous unchecked expenses, court cases, and outstanding receivables, the daily functional rule of our country was returned for local political control with oversight by a United Kingdom appointed governor in 2012. I was introduced to politics by my mother at an early age, but became more familiar during marriage number one, and college. In college I was the Gulf Coast Regional Representative for the American Association of Community Colleges, Student Government President, Vice President, and Senator, respectively. Through piqued interests I learned that my constituency (The Bight, Providenciales) would require representation as the former standard bearer was not available to stand for consideration.

If you know me, you know that I am a supporter of my party, and I do not switch every election cycle because my party did not deliver on their party manifesto or plans that will gravely affect the lives of its people. Yoo- Hoo me, fear was not a factor then, so in gest fashion, I wrote a letter to the Progressive National Party, General Secretary asking to be considered as a candidate and standard bearer in the upcoming General Elections to be held in 2012 at the time. My letter was accepted, I became the candidate for the Bight Constituency, Electoral district number six, and I did not realize until that moment what this entailed.

I had to learn to campaign, which meant going from home-to-home soliciting support and votes at the polls. I had to sacrifice my citizenship as a Bahamian because at the time the Attorney General Chambers misinterpreted the law on who qualified to stand for elections in Turks and Caicos Islands. As a person with dual citizenship this meant that I had to renounce my allegiance to one commonwealth country, for the other.

I was exposed to a much in-depth degree of campaign financing and had to gain the skills necessary to look for and receive funding from strangers, and to set up and articulate my platform and responses to current issues. I had to learn how to speak to an audience larger than a Sunday school class on Sunday. I had to learn how to fight for appropriations that would help me receive the level of support in campaign to garner the votes needed to win. This season was good practice and eventually fear became my fuel from God that he was working on my behalf, and to just simply trust Him. Whether it was sunshine or rain when the assurance came, I was given the strength to do it.

Another moment of fear and there were many, but this one more recent. In February 2019, I found myself in the seat of Pastor as my pastor had died young at seventy years old. The congregation at the time was on average 49 years old as the youngest and the oldest 102 years. Shhhh!!! That was an experience; I had no knowledge of the role internally, only what I saw externally. The examples were not near enough to me to be emulated and a group of people were depending on me. In obedience I trusted God, pulled up my big girl britches, and pressed forward citing everyday Isaiah 54:17 and Philippians 4:13.

Rewards

"Blessed is the man that walketh not in the counsel of the ungodly, nor standeth in the way of sinners, Nor sitteth in the seat of the scornful.... for he shall be a tree planted by the rivers of water, that bringeth forth its fruit in its season" Psalms 1:1KJV.

Communities are the bedrock upon which many individuals survive, and I was so grateful for the one I inherited. To me it can also be described as the birthplace of culture aligned with genetics and practices found in communities. Sabrina, Carrie, Joyce, and Essie were the sisters that I inherited since moving to the United States, and they caused my village to be better as an immigrant. I was focused, I did not come to make friends, I came to matriculate and leave. These ladies' inclusion made me reevaluate my value and see life from different lenses. The outpouring of love and respect, the input of unbiased perspectives, the commitment and dedication to prosperity made our transition hopeful. These ladies cried, laughed, and allowed me to be their big sister on this journey (yes BIG sister) and in return I hope that I returned the love for them in the times they needed me too.

An experience such as this was strangely unfamiliar since I have no sisters from my mom and only met my dad's other daughters, except the one that is deceased, on paper recorded in his Bible upon his death. Small island states are challenging in this degree as most inhabitants are relatives, and when you are limited to siblings, the inclusion is filled with chivalry. Nevertheless, the goal of many is to ensure that their legacy is still consistent with the growth of the country and will be forever etched in the annals of history. Though there were many interruptions during this period they do not outweigh the immeasurable favors. The foundation set by my ancestors giving endlessly to others who were in need or not even family paved a path for me. My children and I were surrounded by love and unity which kept me focused.

Favor was so real I became a homeowner in the United States of America before I earned residency. One Thanksgiving Day in 2000, while having lunch with Essie and her family, she had a sister,

Tommie, that was a real estate agent, and they were discussing the path to homeownership. Inquisitively, I asked lots of question and while the journey was not an easy one, but as favor would have it, God allowed me to be at the right place at the right time, in a temporary – fulltime assignment that supplied sufficient income for approval. I became a homeowner in the United States of America after living here for two years. Tell me God is not real! He continues to bless us even when we sometimes do not deserve it.

She got it from her Mama

My daughter, Eurydice was always an A student and a model student that most of her teachers commented on in her reports and acknowledged that she was the kind of student every teacher prefers. Confrontation was never an attribute that she magnified and in doing so she kept herself remarkably busy with schoolwork and writing. Any time there was an after-school event that involved awards and special programs it was because she was a part of it. One of her music teachers from Best Elementary often requested her to sing the Negro National Anthem at functions outside of work hours, because of her extraordinarily strong second soprano voice.

In 1999, I was awarded a scholarship to study in the United States through the Lyford Cay Foundation at the Houston Community College System. I enrolled in the program; that was the easy part. Staying in the program was a challenge. The composition of students in the class was seventy percent immigrants, and we all knew that to gain a green card to the United States through employment ensured us a lifetime of opportunities that we would not be privy to in our own country. So, the competition was real. We had to make the top five to even be considered by recruiters. Despite the challenges, my academic prowess earned me western hemisphere waivers and endowment scholarships that helped with the cost of my education. I remain grateful.

However, not only in academics did she make me proud but in life's journey. Her tenacity to succeed despite life's challenges causes me to remain in awe of her as a human being. On her 25th birthday she received the most devastating news any child could imagine. On social media, people posted condolences to her in innocence and ignorance. Evan Conrad was the joy of her heart and the first love she ever knew. He was not the perfect father, but he was her father. Overwhelmed by the news, she phoned me and asked what people were talking about. As soberly as I could, I confirmed to my daughter what I had known for a few hours – her father was missing while waiting for confirmation only to be later informed that he was found dead.

Statistically suicide deaths have increased by 36% from 2000 – 2021 according to CDC. [9]Suicide is death caused by injuring oneself with the intent to die. Many factors can increase the risk for suicide or protect against it. Suicide is connected to other forms of injury and violence. For example, people who have experienced violence, including child abuse, bullying, or sexual violence have a higher suicide risk. Being connected to family and community support and having easy access to healthcare can decrease suicidal thoughts and behaviors.

Devastating events cause humans to either live or die. Eurydice chose to live, but she did it her way. Through therapy, and God's grace she continues to thrive as an entrepreneur and makes each day count as she regains complete emotional wellness.

---

[9] (Centers for Disease Control and Prevention, 2023)

Visit to Texas Capital

Annually since 1966 the Texas Senate celebrates "Governor for the Day" by selecting one of their colleagues from the House of Representatives or the Senate to serve as Governor. My friend Essie Jessie whom I met while attending College Park Baptist Church was a journalist, in her younger years and continued working as a public relations representative, what is now renamed content creator/marketing strategists. Essie had three lovely kids, Britney, Jacoby, and Jessica; as well as two sisters Tommie and Bobbie and her dad (I cannot remember his name) who passed not long after we met. I guess early on Essie recognized my passion for politics and people and introduced me to events that made my stay in Houston comfortable.

Such events, including the 'Governor for the Day,' helped me to not miss home as much as most people and allowed me to explore the opportunities that my unfamiliar environment provided. So, on April 8, 2000, my children along with others boarded a bus to Austin Texas to see the momentous occasion of Senator Rodney Ellis being sworn in as Governor for the Day. This trip was an adventure and an educational experience. Yet, another proud moment for the African American diaspora of the constituents of the 13th district in Houston, that Senator Ellis represented from 1990 – 2017. All along I was being prepared for a later journey in my life and did not even realize it. The constituents were proud and showed up in numbers to celebrate the occasion.

The amazing part of me and Essie's friendship was that there was nothing too good for her to share with me and my family. We PRAYED a lot together, had Thanksgiving dinners, birthday parties, and school outings together. She even threw a graduation party for me after my graduation with an associate degree in Electronics Engineering – Biomedical Science from Houston Community College System. In return, I supplied unsolicited advice, prayers and good ole Bahamian cooking especially when my mom visited. Now grant it, I am not the best cook, but I could save a life.

Minute Maid Park

In Turks and Caicos Islands before my transition to the United States of America, there were opportunities for sports, but it did not include baseball. We had Softball, Cricket, basketball, and soccer. Carrie changed that as well as some other things for my family and me. Carrie was first class, a Christian, and an overall servant leader. Carrie worked for Minute Maid, a subsidiary of the Coca Cola Company and God strategically placed her in executive offices where favor was not just fear. Carrie and I met at College Park Baptist Church, and she at the time continues to advocate for a life in Christ Jesus to all she meets.

Minute Maid Park was renamed Astros Field on February 27, 2002, by agreement of the Houston Astros and Enron Corp. Guess what yawl, my children and I along with Carrie and her sons David and Jeremiah could often be found in a clubhouse watching the game at Minute Maid Park. "Look at God." God not only used Carrie for entertainment in our lives, but he also allowed her to teach me how to navigate credit and consumer lending in Texas, of which I was able to buy my first home.

My experiences lead me to believe that the value that favor and fear bring contributes to plans being thought of or constructed on our behalf in the heavenlies. Favor and fear play an integral role in one's success. Without a vision people perish, according to the

Bible. I will continue to believe that favor empowers, and fear makes aware; one thrives on goals that are carefully articulated. Many of us are reliant on both, and we must respond, or we will succumb to societal pressures.

AMAZING

"And the LORD, he it is that doth go before thee; he will be with thee, he will not fail thee, neither forsake thee: fear not, neither be dismayed" <u>Deuteronomy 31:8 (KJV)</u>.

The compassion one receives in the journey of love dims the evil aurora that abandonment presents. In 2 Thessalonians 2:3 (NIV) we read: *"Do not let anyone deceive you in anyway, for that day will not come until the rebellion occurs and the man of lawlessness is revealed; the doomed to destruction"*. The curse of abandonment is designed to ensure that your mindset is aware that the decision of your future has been decided. The experience of growing up without parents present in the home was all too familiar and one parent that was so strict that you could feel the coals of hell's fury while being scolded. That was no joke. As a mature individual a certain level of understanding can be entertained surrounding this notion, but growing up as the second oldest grandchild of my family meant that my dolls were my company when my parents could afford one.

As well the opportunities to make new friends were priceless, so I learned to advocate, lobby, and campaign early. These valuable lessons worked well externally, teaching me social skills, communication, language, and style.

Abandonment, abuse, whatever it is called, disconnects focus and it may be safe to say abandonment amplifies the mental health of an individual. Growing up as a young girl with no sisters, I experienced fatigue, frustration, and fear, and I believed that being able to share them with someone other than an adult would have helped. The absence of support prolonged my ability to recognize the presence of mental Illness, and in many instances, I overdosed on staying busy. During these periods of loneliness and isolation target our vulnerability and our energetic mindset. I am of the view that the right mindset sustains mental toughness and survival skills hopefully affecting positively towards creativity and innovation. Negativity was the order of the day on my mom's side of the family, while on my father's adopted side there were tons of secrets.

In my experience, families, if they have the ability, should strive not to accommodate negative experiences in so much as fear, frustration, and mental erosion in life, at least not as early as was the story of my dad. Christie never spoke of the abandonment, but he expressed it in his actions towards my mom and my brother a lot. Jeffery in hindsight was verbally abused by my father often and never given the opportunity to be a child. I remember when Jeffery completed high school, just to get away from Daddy, he joined the police force, and when he had successfully completed the police academy, my dad was not impressed, nor did he attend the graduation. Or at least he did not act like he was a proud parent.

In our home after my parents were separated, my mom was the HNIC (Head Ninja in Charge) and there were many non-negotiable periods. Thus, the state of abandonment unfortunately became a household member colliding with energy, and the adherence to specific core values. My mom did her best, but the enemy of abandonment motivated my brother and I to succeed, although at the time we did not understand.

After the birth of my eldest son, shortly after his two-week anniversary, one morning I tried to get up out of bed and was unable to walk. My mom did not think it was strange until that episode lasted another two weeks, and I bled profusely from the womb. I was rushed to the hospital by the grandmother of my son, who at the time was a friend of my mom. During the examination, the doctor diagnosed that an error was made during the delivery, and as a result I was still carrying the bag from the birth which caused excessive bleeding, smell, weakness and mobility issues. I was rushed to the operating room where the placenta was removed. After a short hospital stay and a long recovery of another four months I could walk again.

You never know your identity unless there is a need to use it. The surgery removed the placenta and stopped the bleeding, but it did not correct the mobility. My dad, in his wisdom, and nature surmised after several doctor visits that I was harmed in every way through evil practices. Now, can you imagine the surprise, suffering, and sacrifice at my expense, that I experienced. I was emotionally traumatized by the whole ordeal, and this issue was the catalyst for being introduced to witchcraft and voodoo practices. My parents made the decision to support me and my son but not without my surrender of my rights.

My Father, having deep ties to a religion where evil was celebrated more than good, began acting in a manner I had never known. The trip to Haiti was a first for me. We landed in Cape Haitian in 1987 early March. I was afraid; I could not speak the language, my son was only 4 months old, and to my surprise my father spoke, and could understand creole better than English. I saw mountains. I saw rituals of witchcraft cleansing; I saw people being left by families with a hope of being healed in witchcraft hospitals, with an endless bill that could never be repaid alive. This was not a lifestyle; I was accustomed to it. My parents were Bahamians, and no one except my grandmother's maternal stepbrother was Haitian.

I left Haiti two weeks later, at least 5 pounds lighter than I arrived, still incapable of walking on my own, and with an enlightened experience of the Voodoo culture and religion. No information or sign from my dad that that was where he was born, and that my heritage was in that country.

The End before the Beginning

The heading refers to my "Woman at the Well" experiences. The intent of individuals to commit themselves to a relationship which extends to marriage means that the desire for hope is that no one expects to get a divorce. Sadly, this is not the case for a lot of people. Many views marriage as having more than a partner against the grain of the institution and more to the culture that they live in. There are cultures that allow more than one marriage partner but not where I am from, instead we have a cultural practice called "sweet hearting," and when it is challenged you are viewed as the one that has a problem.

My encounter with this cultural practice stems from my parents' marriage which influenced my own behavior later in life. My dad was "sweet hearting", one lady for 29 years until his death, and many more before her with whom he had children. My own experience came when I married Evan, and his version was I committed this act before he did by obeying the Bishop of the Church of God of Prophecy by removing a ring that he bought and put on my finger during our wedding (that story you will read further). The act that I committed was not done so in agreement, and so his excuse to "sweetheart" with a person that he eventually married and produced four other children was because of that incident. Laugh aloud, yes! (He mussy think he was married to his ma aye!)

From my own experience counseling is helpful, resourceful, and recommended pre marriage and post marriage, but is not taken serious in some West Indian communities. Instead, people relegate their emotions only to insinuate that they believe they know more than those that had gone on before us. Wrong, wrong, get marital counseling, people. It is a make-or-break situation, and it supplies resources to help you make wiser decisions going forward. Or you will end up like me, March 10, 1993, standing in the docket of the Supreme Court of the Turks and Caicos Islands asking to be divorced from husband number one due to adultery. Although my parents lived separated lives, divorce was never a possibility for them, and my father died being married to my mother. Just imagine, Judgment Day that was like the atmosphere of the Supreme Court on that day; it was cold and calculated, the climate was frosty, and the employees were stoic in the execution of their duties.

Yet in the annals of those halls humor slipped in while waiting. The couple that went before me was most dramatic in nature. I saw the female was in the parking lot practicing her response on the outside before taking the docket. Practicing her response was what she called her side of her story, and in my view gaining a divorce under false pretenses. My turn came and I wailed like it was a funeral. I was scared and I cried. I was hurt, embarrassed and tired so I pushed through and answered three questions: 1. When did the marriage break down? 2. Did you receive marital counseling? 3. Do you still want to be divorced today? In tears my response, one year later, adultery, no, and yes. I felt abandoned. Lessons learned from this event, however, were insufficient to deter me from accepting marriage again.

Marriage Number One

Weddings are a celebration signifying a marriage has begun, just that. According to the traditional vows, and I paraphrase Marriage entered unwisely is an expensive mistake, and once focus is no longer present it can become a nightmare for all involved.

April 1, 1989, was a beautiful day. It was colorful, cheerful, expensive, and filled with friends, family and excitement that affected the small community of Kingstown, Providenciales at that time. The Bight girl was being joined in matrimony to the boy from Blue Hills whose father was a prominent figure, and from a reputable family. Despite the happiness of the day, the joy in the relationship soon died between those being joined. Remember, I said what is not entered into wisely can someday become a thorn in your side. Well suffice it to say the signs and secrets were there. I am not sure he knew, but my grandmother Rose at one time mentioned something surrounding a violation that happened between families, but I ignored it; I was in love.

The thing is there was no stewardship in the marriage, and we failed. Both of us abandoned the principles that guided what was ordained. We acknowledged the presence of counseling, and we ignored the chatter of trusted and hated individuals. Or did they know more than we and laughed behind our backs? Also never use rejection as ammunition to enter another relationship.

The marriage ended exactly twelve months after the commencement and the divorce started March 1993. From that relationship I had my second child, a girl. There was no model of divorce for me to follow, but there were examples of survival. This was my interpretation of it, and I chose this route. Here Comes the Bride again...

By the year 2000, even though I enjoyed the community within the southern Baptist church I attended, I needed and wanted to grow spiritually with people who were my color and had a familiar worship style. This was not easy for me or my children as they had just become familiar with where we were, and my son, Cobreti, was beginning to earn a little money for playing the drums. But it was time to go; we ought not always go by our feelings – the outcome could be robbery.

I began attending a new church which I will call Hallelujah Dominance, a non-denominational charismatic church about a three-minute drive from where I stayed on Beechnut Street, in Houston Texas. At that time, they met in an elementary school before buying property. The Pastor was young and energetic, and he knew how to navigate them homiletics to soothe your soul. There I enjoyed the fellowship, but my children were never able to make friends like the ones that they had at the other church. I on the other hand became a member and was a regular volunteer in the office and trained to become a lay preacher.

Never mix water with fire because one of them will stop working. It was time to date again, and I had met a calm, collective and handsome gentlemen whose genealogy (Turks and Caicos Island and the Bahamas) was like mine, and we shared lots of things in common, or so I thought. One thing led to another and as a female attracted to a male, a pregnancy happened, and I got married for the second time in July 2003. This union lasted a total of sixteen years, but the marriage was over eighteen months after it began. Without a doubt love existed in the marriage; agape was fully present, but not in the way two consenting adults should display to one another in a marriage. In my view, anytime something drains you of your peace it is time to let that go; ending December 2018.

Friendships

My friends are so unique. You will find them all spread out in the arenas of church and politics, members, and constituents. Can I positively suggest that they too feel as if I am invaluable to them; Friendship is a commodity, and an extension of God's presence.

Debbie #1, Debbie #2, Rhonda, Phillippa, Cindy, Monica, Karen, Chantarelle, Delena, Dellareese, Joy, Hilary, Sabrina, Joyce, Carrie, Essie, Dominica, Kelcine, Denyce, Yvette, Kendall, and Nora. Like seasons, all these names and for some reason I am going to get in trouble by naming people, each one of them significantly contributed to my life in one way or another. From high school Debbie #2, Rhonda, Phillippa, Cindy, and Monica were my besties, one of these ladies ended up marrying one of the guys I dated; and we are still best friends after 38 years and she is also godmother to my eldest son.

Twenty friends are a lot for one person to have and certainly does not support the cliché "small circle," except these people are to be commended for sticking around and putting up with me. In true Gemini fashion, before they can finish a sentence or project on one topic with me, I have transitioned to another topic. Often, I am cited by anyone of them as being bi-polar in nature, but the truth is I get bored quickly and therefore the amusement in these relationships is in my own hands, instead of vice versa. The thing is, I value my time here on earth and I am extremely intentional in my actions.

Intentionality sometimes brings clarity to life situations, and each of my friends supplied me with the energy to continue. Although their lives were filled with their own responsibilities, they found time for me.

UNUSUAL

"And the peace of God, which passeth all

understanding, shall keep your hearts and minds

through Christ Jesus" <u>*Philippians 4:7 (KJV)*</u>.

Understanding

There was a revival at the local church I attended at the time on McCullough Corner in Nassau Bahamas, I was around 14 or 15 years old as I remember and the preacher spoke in syllables and words that were not English, interpreted tongues. I remember sitting on the bench with my friends giggling because to us it was funny, and so we mocked the evangelist. What my friends did not know because I hid it from them with a foolish prank preceding the laughter was that night, I received the Holy Ghost as it were.

Evangelist: Young people come to the altar, the Lord is soon to return, and you do not want to be caught without Christ."

Young people (including myself): Ha Ha right!

In reluctance, cross eye from our parents, and the prompting of the spirit of God to the obedience of the evangelist call, we walked slowly to the altar, with smirks, thoughts, and lots of doubt. The evangelist who was a gentleman prayed for our ignorance first, forgiveness, and then asked us to extend our hands to the sky, and to repeat the sinner's prayer, and we did. That went something like this:

"Lord Jesus please come into my life, forgives me of all my sins, cleanse me. I want to be your child, make me new. Fill me with your Holy Ghost, in Jesus Name."

All of us standing at the altar did so, and what happened next, gave hope to the church, the body of Christ, and our parents. To the apostolic movement, demonstrations or acts of spiritualism are sure signs that one has received the power of the Holy Spirit. Some of us began to dance and sing, and others speak in other tongues. I had to be carried from the altar; I fell out and woke up speaking a language not in English. The revelation as I now see it was at that time, more aware of the importance of the power of God, and His servants who are trusted with such assignments. This was my introduction to church, ministry, and Christianity.

At fifteen years old, my official journey in Christendom had begun, regular Bible readings, lots of church functions, and watching families be molested and abused in the name of God, and Church. These years saw many of my acquaintances straight jacketed into relationships and perspectives that minimized their potential as human beings. For example, we had to conform to practices interpreted by several men of the then ministry as doctrine. Here I began to learn about serving others in need, and supporting those less desired, especially in areas where the people you serve were the cause of your pain.

As an adult I later learned or believed that the concept of Christianity looked to aid one is being eradicate from social ills that may look to destroy your profitable future or enhance a deteriorating outcome. I was Christian since I was 15 years of age, rocking to the rhythms of some good ole gospel Caribbean music, the order of the day. My brother and I could be found in church activities at least 3 times a week, i.e., band practice, young people's meeting, and Sunday school. We idolized some of our other friends that we saw living in Christian homes.

What we did not realize at the time the mystery, of the unlimited supply to what God has in store if we are obedient not distracted. All we must do is commit our ways to him according to Hosea 12:6, "Ask, Seek, and Knock" and walk through the door when the opportunity becomes available.

The difference stands out when you realize that each assignment offers lessons that could not be found in the other. One such lesson is that of becoming a mother. I have had 3 live births and one foster. I reference each of them to the directions on the earth: East. West, North, and South. There are no two alike, each having their own minds and abilities. As a parent I had to learn quickly or I would find myself being clueless in managing each of them, in needs, character, and wants.

There is unlimited potential in recognizing who one is and being aware while thriving in growth as an individual one must consciously address the issues that will broaden their ability to take part and remain competitive. Unlimited access to knowledge, position, and resource will place you in the position where doors will open. Having a mentor, coach, or counselor is also helpful.

Having the will to listen to good advice allows things to flow freely on your behalf. For example, scholarships that you would not have otherwise qualified for without guidance, being given a car by a stranger after moving to a city where you knew absolutely no one, and worshipping at a church because after you prayed, God sent direction, and you followed. Like the famous credit card commercial on MasterCard – PRICELESS!

Cobreti, my son would always refer to his sister Eurydice, as a book worm, while describing her as the academia of the family. During one of his birthdays, he was asked by a relative what he wanted for a gift, he said, "surely not a book, that's for my sister, she is the nerdy one." Today he is the husband to Therese, father of beautiful daughters (Aniyah, and Imani), and a dog (Nola), and an aviation mechanic, that travels six months a year overseas for work. That took some level of studying, and commitment to achieve, I think. As his mother I am truly proud of him, and continually pray that the Lord would guard his heart and mind always.

Unlimited

Moving forward is critical, and to everything there is a season under the heavens, so says the Bible. The Bible also suggests that there are more for us, than those against us. Provocative gestures illustrate the potency of what being undermined by those close to you can do. In secular cultures the cleanup left on aisle nine is left to the custodians of the building. Those who did the undoing are often long gone and take no responsibility for their actions. What do I mean, my parents were my first leaders when I was born, but as leaders their armor had lots of dents, due to the battles that they faced.

My journey to college was filled with hope but laced with hitches along the way. I was awarded three scholarships before the dream could be manifested, and when I took the leap, it was because of a partial not full scholarship. My grades from high school were of the least quality but the God that I serve had unlimited supply, and according to Ephesians 3:8, I am unworthy, but he chose me to show his endless supply, as they say the rest is history. The bountifulness of God extended to my family as well is simply amazing.

Meanwhile, character is what sustains anything and anywhere one is placed. Character is a threat to undoing making the nature of an individual, intents, and paths they choose tread well whilst achieving outcomes, a subscription to unusual and unseemly acts that do not necessarily reflect an agape style of love and life. What am I saying? How does this relate to what is being discussed? You see my mom knew I was a leader from the onset, and despite what I endured as an individual, she kept reminding me that the only important thing was what God would say about me in the end, as He is the author of our stories.

I had many opportunities to be immoral, one of which was discovering that my brother's death was not of his own volition, but the evil intent and selfish acts of others. Also, I had a child out of wedlock. I aborted four babies. My brother was infected with HIV/AIDS at a tender age, and his hopes and dreams died and were buried too early, at the age of twenty-seven (27) years. To allow God to take revenge for you is a lesson. I wanted to act, but God's way is always the better way.

What I now realize in life is that unsavory behaviors are common to a desperate leader whose journey is provoked. My brother loved them; they claimed to love him but did not show their health status to him and his life was cut short. While these paths were all painful, I did not allow any of those discretions to forge the path for my future.

The scenes were inspirational enough to be cruel, criminal and careless, but God was instrumental in his love toward me at every turn. Instead, I chose to forgive the ones who left me to raise my son on my own. I forgave the men that gave me monies to abort unborn babies, and I forgive individuals that were deceptive in their relationships towards my family and me. Instead, I served them.

Undermining

To undermine is a negative connotation that supports dishonesty, jealousy, envy, and wrongdoing. Unfortunately, I have experienced this in my personal life, church, work, and politics; the price you pay for growth. Stories of these acts in leadership are all too familiar and with real time examples that examine, and that could influence your ability to lead. My own experience caused me to see that successful leadership is not complete unless undermining techniques justify the outcome based on the goal set.

In 2002, I interviewed for a full-time position at Houston Community College System, as an enrollment associate and the question I was asked was something like this: 'what are your future career plans?' In haste, not clearly thinking I answered, "to become a leader in politics in my country." I had been preparing for a life in politics my entire life, but never allowed myself to entertain the idea without being coerced. My dream was to stand for people, not in the halls of the House of Assembly but in the courtroom as a lawyer.

Nothing happens without work, and I completed applications to universities in the UK and Caribbean, to which I received no reply or acceptance. Timing has a role to play in everything. However, I felt as if I was undermined at every turn with only a little strength left to convince the twins in me that it was the loss of any institution who underscored the value of my becoming a member. The energy needed to stay focused was daunting. As a young person, the duplicity of reasons to succeed did not exist, and the reasons to remain stifled were in abundance.

You are wondering what I mean? Just what I said! No formula for success exists without a strategy that undermines the integrity of the outcome. Another experience I have is that of campaigning in an election cycle for any position and winning. My first experience was in college for the position of Senator – Gulf Coast for the American Student Association of Community Colleges of which the Student Government organization of Houston Community College – Central Campus was apart. The opening became available at a conference in 2001, and I was encouraged by my student advisor to apply. Winning but not without compromise.

Most candidates in races somehow enter with the notion that they are capable of their own volition. No, no, no it takes a village. I learned that lobbying, advocating, having a platform, and making promises that you will not be able to keep are normal. What was surprising was the amount disloyalty and untruths that were either hurled at the individual or proposed to the voters to win support.

LIVING WELL

"A good man leaves an inheritance to his children's children."

(NKJV) Proverbs 13:22

What I learned in my lifetime is that in a performance the act proves what you are capable of and able to do based on the script, or impromptu situations. Acts in plays, movies, and documentaries are scripted, but in real life they normally show up uninformed, and with no instructions. Despite the mode of transport, there are lessons to be learned as a leader. Whether it is found in lifestyles, loyalty or listening, there is a lesson. Each of these lessons was significant to my growth as an independent, strong woman looking to navigate my life, and leisure.

What was most significant during the process was my ability to trust, my reliance on my faith in God, and patience to obtain the promise. As intellectual and religious, as that sentence may sound, it was not easy, especially when you are the first in your family to obtain a tertiary level degree, with lots of exposure globally in work and community service. The will to begin the practices and principles that you learned along the way to enhance your perspective requires no physical, mental, or emotional support from those you count worthy. In many ways, this is very discouraging, but my mama tells me often that in life, there will always be differences. Differences not only apply when individuals are compromised in their personal beliefs and standards, but also in familial relationships.

Loyalty

Being loyal is joy wrapped up in prickle bush; that is how exceedingly rare it exists today. The absence of loyalty when going through a test unveils the authenticity of value and relationship in the lives of those being affected. In the workplace one would think that the same expectation exists, except that it is not necessarily true. After being employed with an international bank in 2007, I excelled in promotions over 2 years to the position of branch manager. Each tier of leadership became an integral part of my growth as a leader. The nuance of being new to banking, finance and direct customer service did not sway me enough to not believe that I was not on track to becoming the first local Director of an International Bank in my country at the time. Ah, but this was not the mindset of some including, "Jehovah Nissi – the Lord my Banner" whose vision of me included ensuring that I would never take that seat.

The plot thickened, and I was fired. Yes, you heard right. I enjoyed promotions. I enjoyed the incentives. I enjoyed empowerment and would recommend a banking career to anyone, but it was not written on the cards for my future. Hence on September 11, 2011, I was fired as a Branch Manager of a bank. I remember my supervisor, arriving at the branch that I worked at, asking me to meet in my office. Giving me a talk, that made absolutely no sense, and completely un-factual. Next, he asked me for the keys, and the phone, and then instructed me to clean out my personal items.

Where was the loyalty here? Where was the support that loyalty is supposed to bring? After the many speeches, and talks, "I will support you in every decision you make as a manager," "I got your back". Guess what? There was none. Before then, my experience with that kind of loyalty was vague. Leaders, families, associations, team members, and organizations are expected to be loyal to the company they are employed in, or if you are an entrepreneur, it would be your clients and staff. Counting on the process to correct whatever is undone or interrupted.

The atmosphere was rigged with discrimination and prejudice over cloud with a bright future. That day I was fired as a Banking officer, shocked and traumatized me. I had never ever been fired in my life. I was accustomed to being in control of the family situations and surroundings, and not being unprepared. I hate surprises, even birthday parties. The manager who trained me claimed insubordination among other things which could not be proven. One individual's mistake and missteps resulted in a monetary loss to the institution, because I won in the end. Nonetheless the experience taught me the importance of due diligence, the effectiveness of compliance, how to manage people, and the value of ethics.

They Left Me to Die

In 2016, my political party lost the bid to continue being government in the Turks and Caicos Islands. I was the candidate and standard bearer of the constituency (the Bight, ED6) whom before my predecessor, consecutive terms were held by the other party. Also, in that constituency called the Bight often referred to as the "breadbaskct," of the Turks and Caicos Islands, the social classes, are so distinctly visible compared that it is referred to different names (I.e., Grace Bay, the Bight, Leeward Highway). Expectedly, I entered politics hoping to gain some alliances in my own party that would help me to achieve for my constituents the necessary infrastructure to become more productive and successful citizens.

The experience during the general elections was one for the books; I was left like a hanging chard. The votes had been counted and my opponent and I had the same count; the count was done three times, and the results were the same. The election regulations dictated the process to follow in this event, that a chard was drawn between the two highest scoring candidates. So, my opponent and I were informed by the returning officer what to expect. The election official instructed us to print our names on a piece of paper, and to deposit them in the box, and one of them will draw. Whoever's chard was withdrawn first, would be the winner. Well... I won.

Frustrating for me was that no one from the party executive echelon was present for this process. Our party had lost the government, and I am guessing the emotions were low, so people packed up and retired to their homes, and I was alone in the process, or so I thought. The people that supported me from my constituency, and the one stalwart, who answered his phone was concerned about me, and had not given up on the seat or my ability to deliver for my party. My profound opinion at the end of the day was that in this newfound relationship, loyalty only mattered when the vote is counted, and your seat allows your party to be successful in the goal of reaching the government.

Five of us won our seats and became the Opposition. To me, it is the most influential position in any government that is strategically placed to ensure all communities are drastically underserved after the winning party that forms the government is not disenfranchised. In this lesson, I further realized in those positions the level of accountability outranks ignorance and incompetence especially as it pertains to country. Yet, those who walked those halls seldom remember the impact of LOYALTY to voters/constituents emotionally and they return every four years to do the same walk all over again.

Lifestyles

I understand lifestyles as being in adoption, or cultural behaviors based on traditions, and practices which dictate that you accommodate and entertain what is necessary to develop. To me, this makes humans believe that we owe the living and the dead. My grandmother, Rose was an exceptionally beautiful light skinned woman, proud, and depended on her God to answer and deliver her from all life experiences that she considered were unbearable; therapy at those times in her life came from wise women of wisdom, or the Bible. The importance of God as I said earlier signified the level of commitment my family had to religion.

Owning or having a home was a luxury and the ownership of the property legally was not a crucial factor. Families from all cultures take pleasure in living in proximity to each other, and on parcels of land that is owned by a parent, grandparent, or family until recently. Upon my return in 2006 to the Turks and Caicos Islands, I grew worried about this reality, and the security of my family's physical legacy so I manipulated the landscape of this ideal by stressing to my relatives the security of what they were gifted. Every child of my grandmothers, including my mom, was allotted a piece of property from their mom, as an inheritance. These allotted plots at transfer would value around $45k which meant that each recipient would be in possession of an asset with no liability. A legacy most people dream about and one all of us should be considering when we imagine inheritance for our children.

What was also frustrating was the lack of education and awareness that this kind of lifestyle could mean and be able to do for an individual not accustomed to managing wealth at any level. So, I had to get to work, tackling mindsets, and grooming. I approached my aunts, sold them the idea of owning their property. Everyone agreed, but the funds to ensure the process happened trickled in slowly. Back then, I wished YouTube and social media platforms were more popular especially since they help in supplying several aspects and interpretations for various issues.

Once the legal process was completed, the tensions subsided, and the awareness increased as to the possibilities this provided. I am just grateful that the example taught me to never take anything for granted, especially family.

Listening

"Don't do what I do, do what I tell you to do", a line often repeated by my mother, but not often an example set. This was a statement that I constantly ignored as a child and as an adult. Until recently, once I acknowledged you in some way, or communicated with you, I was listening. I further found out that listening is critical to life's choices.

I am a friendly person, and I was warned that friendships in politics do not exist; boy did I miss that message. Friendships in all genres of society are extremely rare and are not to be expected in your personal life, business, and as a leader. A tough lesson, but one learned sooner. I am an entrepreneur who sold Avon during college and consulted while obtaining my undergraduate degree which helped me to pay bills. Currently, at the writing of this book as an insurance agent, listening to clients who continue to convince themselves that they are prepared for the demise of their loved ones financially without checking the cost is key.

Likewise in all forms of leadership wherever success is derived it comes through hard work, collaboration, and cooperation. Listening is a key part to understanding direction, career and life goals. If you do not master this, you will fail at being and doing whatever you set out to do. My career goal was to become a lawyer, not reached; I listened to my boyfriend, who later left me for another woman. I became a mother, and my goal was amended to fit life's current situation.

Teamwork makes the dream work and during my first campaign for political office in the Turks and Caicos Islands, I had a dynamic and phenomenal team, and in 2013, I failed, and I did not listen. Kudos to them and thank you; I will not call names, but I remain forever grateful. Due to the landscape and the stakeholders, the wisdom provided by these volunteers was exceptional and the level of passion for country and politics were outmatched. Do not get me wrong, there were some wolves in sheep's clothing, but the sheep outshined them.

The circulation of a newsletter to constituents to keep them abreast of how I was being their voice in the halls of parliament, as well as what was next on my agenda vital to the sustainability of the lives of the citizens in those communities, was the plan. It was an excellent idea, but in true Porsha style, and I enjoy sharing ideas, resulted in the first draft of the newsletter completed but never published, or printed for distribution. To me this was an active participant in the narrow escape at the polls in 2016, I undervalued my constituents, disrespected them, learned many lessons in people management and the rest, as they say is history. I won a second term by one vote, the drawing of a chard, yes, you read right, and a court case. I won by one vote.

Unfortunately, as an individual desirous of growth and development for positive change, the ride to the top is filled with thorns and roses. Thorns that will supply opportunities for growth and roses that will influence your comfort level if you are happy where you are. The choice is yours to decide.

TRANSFORMATION

"Therefore, if any man is in Christ, he is a new creature, old things are passed away behold all things become new." 2 Corinthians 5:17

"We shall be changed; we shall be changed from mortal to immortality in the twinkling of an eye." This song, I learned as a child, was sung by a famous male group called the Cooling Waters in the Bahamas. I know that it is Biblically (1 Corinthians 15: 52) based and a fan favorite, perfect song to begin my thoughts on transformation. Transformation demands change; transformation dictates that our mindset includes the willingness to be open to innovative ideas and possibilities. [10]Transformation advocates for change, and in most instances, there is a leader and a follower. The focus of transformation is to engage followers at a level unfamiliar to reach a standard. In humanity we are conditioned as being enslaved, working hard for everything we need or want. But what

---

[10] Northouse, Peter, (2019) Leadership

happened to the message that we continue to hear in church and motivational messages from people that say we can have that and more? No mention of labor in all instances just speaking.

Change is a game changer and those who are not receptive to change often discover that the lack of not knowing and reaching is sometimes more daunting than the process of change itself. I wanted to be different; I pushed myself to limits that were unheard of or even tried by any of my kin. When given the opportunity to sit at tables, I did not shy away; I sat even if I only picked up a few words that were key and essential to the conversations. In 1996/7, I was elected chairperson of the local committee of Persons Living with Aids and HIV in Providenciales, and later the Vice Chairperson of the same group for the Turks and Caicos Islands.

In both roles I stood for Turks and Caicos Islands at various high-level meetings on the dialogue of this then unknown and intriguing disease, and at the time I was only a high school graduate with a technical certificate in Air Conditioning and Refrigeration. My background in academia was not sufficient but my experience prepared me for the journey. My brother was one of the first in line of persons from Turks and Caicos Islands that contracted the disease, and while others were afraid due to stigma to talk about or be associated publicly, I took on the challenge and by the grace of God, gained knowledge, and championed awareness for those in need. The group along with the Ministry of Health ensured that the best care and medication for the citizens and residents affected was received and distributed.

Most believe that only people living in poverty or less than conditions require transformation. Poverty limits humans except in spiritual nature. (see Matthew 5:3) There it matters most, where they are promised to experience the kingdom of heaven in fullness. The beatitudes are promises made by Jesus in a Sermon on the Mount, and one which we repeated in Sunday school every Sunday as children. There is hope after all. There is an assurance that transformation would restore and give life to dead situations.

For such, growing up poor was not to be frowned on but commended. The feeling of being trampled on, abused (mentally, physically, sexually), is not sensual or attractive, but it is against such backdrops in which transformation occurs. My desire was and still is to make a difference in other people's lives, and mine. The desire not to contribute never crossed my mind as a single mother, a divorced woman, a fired employee, a battered woman, or even as servant of the people.

Yet in all, Maturity helps, and TIME breathes lessons which implode wisdom nuggets. The journey required me to give more than I expected when entering relationships and experience the gift and peace of God. John 15:9 states *"if you belonged to the world, it would love you as its own."* I was not the world to love, but I was put here to love the unlovable.

He Set Me Free

All my life the examples of living a good life were modeled through deeply religious examples relegating that being spiritual was more fruitful than being fiscally comfortable. I was christened in a Lutheran church. As a child, I attended Southern Baptist church with my grandmother when my parents had to work and engaged in Sunday school and youth activities. At the age of nine years old I was introduced to the Pentecostal style of worship in adult life. During my adult life, I married a talking Anglican and later returned to the Apostolic/Pentecostal style of worship. I have been a church hopper from the beginning. Instability was deeply rooted in me from the start to my adult life Whew! Throughout my adult life it became more visible, and in meditation I found myself regretful for decisions that were made.

I was open minded, or so I thought. I enjoyed adventure and was curious about why as Christians our stance was different from others. In response I delved into and rebelled. I was not my parents; I was in church. I did not drink, smoke, carouse, have extramarital affairs and I tithed. Tithe was all I could do; making an offering above that amount was not possible. I worked two jobs. I was home at midnight for my children after I had a relationship with someone that was not my husband. In physical view, I was not my parents. I was transformed, because every Sunday I got up, and took my children to church, took part on the Praise Team, taught Sunday school, and if I was off on a Wednesday night, I went to Bible study and prayer meeting. I could act well, totally dismissing the power of a relationship with God, and doing my own thing.

I thank God for servants like my Pastor, Rev. Dr. David McDonald Stubbs (deceased 2018). A man worthy of double honor as the scripture alludes to via the Holy Bible. He was a humble, diligent, strong-willed man and a theological genius. You see, Pastor Donald was as some may choose to describe him a warrior. For 26 years he led the formerly Pentecostal Baptist Church now Pentecostal Restoration Centre as teacher, exhorter, prophet, preacher, and father. I remember quite clearly when He was given this assignment how hesitant he was. I was not sure at that time why, but as time went on and I began to learn the man called and chosen by God, and the reason. You see some may have seen him as gap filler then, but he understood the assignment from the onset and was ready to work.

During his tenure, the church flourished, and it weaned. During the flourishing days of his ministry, I counted at least 12-14 ministries/ churches that were born from his tutelage. Yes, I said under his leadership. I saw teachers, prophets, preachers, politicians, business owners all due to him not compromising the word of God and standing up for holiness in whatever season we were in. The ministry was one of the first on the island to set up a school under his leadership for children in K-6th grades, also aligning with international networking partners of other non-denominational evangelical ministries throughout Canada, the USA, and the Caribbean Region.

Pastor Stubbs had a way of telling you that it was God's way, or you can hit the Highway! He was not about the things of this world except his family. He would say to me at times, "Sis. Porsha, I am not going to hell for them, so you know!" Pastor was persistent in his call to ministry. He endured hardness as a good soldier even though his physical body kept screaming loudly in his ears for him to stop. On my returning to the congregation in the last 4 years before his passing my Pastor was happy, and assured me often that whatever his lot, God had taught him to say, "It is Well!"

Pastor was a chef. He served his home, children, spouse, and those around him often with savory dishes made by his hands, for example my favorite conch and rice below. He enjoyed seafood endlessly and spoke often how his wife enjoyed the way he prepared these dishes. My two older children, Rudolph and Courtnee gave their lives to God under his ministry. My eldest, Rudolph because of a word spoken into his life by my Pastor can play any musical instrument that he puts his hands on. My Pastor, when I met him played the guitar, but before he met the Savior face to face deep weeks ago, he was playing the keyboard as well, as the guitar.

I learned about the supernatural from my Pastor. You see three Sundays before his passing we returned to our church to resume full service after experiencing roof damage during Hurricanes of 2017. The last of those 2 Sundays we sat in that building just the two of us and the spoke of his love for the Turks and Caicos, his love for his family, and his love for the body of Christ. As I stated, it was just me and my Pastor on the last Sunday where he properly scolded me because as he termed it, I was being stubborn and resistant to advancing in ministry and the time had come. I again ignored him, brushed him off and he paid me back by preaching to me and the chairs for one hour and twenty minutes.

I was truly annoyed at him and was looking for ways to tell him off like Dec. Eremilda Simons. I was not old enough to get away with it, so I just grumbled to myself, dropped him home and then went home and told my mom about it. My Pastors final sermon to me was to emphatically state that "Faith is the substance of things hoped for and the evidence of things"! He continued to reiterate how we doubt God after we ask, yet we say we are his children and that we repeat often to others that his promises are new every morning and great is his faithfulness. My Pastor proclaimed to me that to love God is to trust Him and to take Him at his word! He admonished me to remain steadfast unmovable always abounding in the form of the Lord… so that my labor would not be in vain. He reminded me that a life of faith is not filled with emotions, but a solid understanding of what God says in his Word is the only thing that we as believers can rely on.

Even with all that wisdom, counsel, and prayers I nearly lost an election in 2016; I lost my home that was less than 5 years from being paid off in 2018. My life was chaotic, because of one wrong interpretation and multiple moves. What was so amazing is that even though I disobeyed, and created my own play cards, God still granted me grace in the process each step ensuring that I was aware that the trump cards and deuce were always in his hands! I lacked the wisdom and the understanding to recognize the new season that was upon me. Thank God His love for me was unwavering.

High School

Transformational leaders influence mindsets and focus on lasting and permanent change. Each dependent on situations and circumstances needed for positive influential situational impacts. In transformation, the shedding of things, ideas, and people that I thought were necessary for my journey made me more focused. Further, based on my research in various places, and my own interpretation, individuals recognize such as transactional not transformational individuals. Many so-called transactional leaders emphasize abilities and focus on outcomes.

This was not the case in high school. In high school we had tons of fun. We did the usual. We missed classes. We skipped school, on the weekends we rode the back of trucks to parties. We had boyfriends, and even borrowed an administrative staff vehicle from time to time to go to the nearest liquor store to pick up our high school drink of choice - Riunite! None of us considered the cost of being transformed into mature women, as at those times it was all about the moment.

Even during my high school years, God was with me, and he did not allow me to die because transformation was possible. I was the follower that had a purpose attached to my life, and the mission could not be aborted due to my reckless lifestyle. Even then John 15:16 declared my life was not my own and I did not realize. "You did not choose me, but I chose you and appointed you so that you might go and bear fruit – fruit that will last ..." I wanted instant gratification and felt that God was moving too slow, and not in the fashion that I imagined.

Waking UP

Discrimination, prejudice, eviction, and promotion pass up are opportunities for transformation to occur in one's life. For me none of these were the motivation that empowered me to prosper or make changes. My life was good, but it was a ghetto. I was just existing and not making a difference. I had successes but I knew that I wanted to prosper in every area of my life. I was known but my legacy was threatened by my behaviors, and mortality. In Luke

22:31, the Lord told Simon, that *"Satan desired to sift him as wheat,"* that is how I felt in 2003. Individuals dismissing the power of what is believed to be negative must be prepared to deal with the consequences. The heartache derived from choices that do not at once return dividends can be detrimental if your faith in God is not strong, and your support group is limited. Life was colorful for me, but in the struggles and trying to figure things out I learned to trust an amazing God.

Finding myself alone, and in isolation made me wake up! Waking up was not fun, it meant that I had to be accountable and responsible. Therapy was not an option because I could not afford it and to date, I am just searching for options as I desperately need it. In my family no one was being anything other than a transactional leader – responding to crisis. I learned as I went. Legacy was important in my journey.

Most of the people that I had the privilege of sitting with, and learned to associate myself with, had no clue that my experience was novice. I had learned to communicate well with others (street trained) by reading and listening. I was going to make it. I was going to be the first in my family to do something different. I was going to "not just exist but make a difference."

To embrace a forward-thinking mindset shows that one thinks and acts beyond the ability or ability to perform. What is most intriguing is the maintenance of this approach while articulating purpose and the creation of a vision. However, being transformed requires an inner work on oneself that goes beyond the surface responsibilities that we see daily. Likewise, evaluation and examination undergird the framework of transformation. Transformation is perpendicular to success and disrupts unilateral dysfunctional responses.

Naturally, I respond well to the cries of community people needing ability in banking, church, and mentorship in life skills can all become like second nature. Answering the call to serve them from a country level was also easy but the work itself there is where the challenge lies. The experience in country governance presented a new and more challenging learning curve. Many days I found myself, cowering due to expectations, exhaustion, and experience. One such occasion occurred when negotiating with a developer that supplied opportunities for employment of locals, while ensuring that locals were not disenfranchised through development concessions access to real property left to them by their ancestors. In this position, the final decision always results in a loss from either one side.

SERVANT LEADERSHIP

"They that have power to hurt and will do none...,"

Shakespeare

Don't be selfish; don't try to impress others. Be humble,

thinking of others as better than yourselves. (Philippians 2:3)

The Servant Leadership philosophy is about leaders with the "[11]desire is to serve first" on their way to becoming or perfecting their leadership skills. This according to Greenleaf comes first as a natural feeling, not a college or continuing education credit class. Most servant leaders appreciate individuals who view change as powerful, and in so doing enslave themselves for the good of others. The philosophy of servant leadership involves introspection, conformity, and perfection. Perceptively it supplies guidance that will groom leaders into becoming self-aware through serving others, through love (examined, evaluated, and experienced) and self-

---

[11] Greenleaf, Robert K. 1991, 2008

143

sacrifice. The core values of servant leadership: [12]Listening, understanding, language, imagination, withdrawal, acceptance, empathy, knowledge, foresight, awareness, healing, belief, and serving ascribe and decide our fortitude to engage in the ministry of love. Love defined by me meant suffering so that the masses (my family) could be restored to humane standards.

I was shaped into being a leader through servanthood at the age of acknowledgement 12 years old and I did the work. Why the age of 12? That is when my eyes opened that my mom was a functional adult that could not read, and my father was street trained, and people took advantage of their illiterate abilities. My mom would credit groceries from a neighborhood store, and sometimes pay double for the items until I realized that she was being robbed. As a result, there were arguments between my parents as to where the money was spent. I took on the task and responsibility of helping them to manage the finances, which allowed my mom to build a money chest of her own for the times when my father became

---

[12] Greenleaf, Robert K. (1999) The Servant as Leader

violent because he was having extramarital affairs, and the abuse of alcohol.

The agony of having to become an adult before even being a child is an experience children should not have to face. Sadly, reality dictates otherwise. I worked early in my life. Work that sometimes caused me so much pain, but based on my reflections, it was more about conviction. Conviction drove my motivation as an individual leader to ensure that followers,' my parents' needs at the time, were met; I served others because they looked like, asked for, and showed a condition for help. From being born into poverty, to being sacrificed in poverty, growing up in poverty, to being recognized in poverty, I served and still do.

How does one tell if they are servant leaders? [13]Theorists contend that mentally when analyzed despite the current environment the result after your presence should dictate a changed atmosphere. In other words, it is designed to stamp out evil and replace it with good. The enemy being identified as the circumstance

---

[13] Greenleaf, Robert K (1999, 2008) The Servant as Leader

not the individual. Like you, I said, "Oh Really!" I grew up with so much hurt and pain that I clearly did not associate or align these experiences with such idealistic expectations. Hurt shaped my posture; it guided my emotional compass to thrive when the options were not aligned with ensuring that I escaped the pain of my present situations.

God provides the Grace to overcome evil with good. We are persuaded in scriptures that this is a result from those of us practicing and following Jesus. As Christians, we are to model this righteous and non-self-judgment behavior. In full disclosure, we are the hands and feet of Christ on earth, so it is our responsibility to affect. Easier said than done but doable; the examples secularly and scripturally already prove that our steps are ordered in service. Despite my unpreparedness for the journey, I trusted God, began putting in the work, and prepared myself for the commencement.

Culturally, it was not a goal based on the society I belonged to. The goals were set so long ago by our ancestors whose foresight did not articulate how to deal with corruption, diversity, and the formulation of mental toughness in the engagement of achieving goals. The scope they imagined was of a peaceful resolution in hopes that all will understand that what they left to us would remain ours if we wanted. Imagine three generations removed and you becoming the leader of the family that will allow them to enjoy their inheritance.

Pressure was the anecdote that powered the energy of moving forward and with each lesson learned, I continued to push forward. I lead my family (inclusive of my immediate relatives), became the caretaker of my brother after his illness, I took care of bills that he left including his daughter. I was changing the atmosphere, and creating legacy during my pain and did not even realize. The goal for me was to escape poverty at all costs leaving no one behind.

I had to filter my emotions for this to take place, and filtering demanded sacrifice, and the ability to LOVE without boundaries. There was no time to entertain my pain, it had to be silent. The goal was not me; it was US (family). Using this approach helps to transform leaders into servants internally and in time it shows externally in their behavior towards followers. The needs of followers are integral in the design to supply real-life examples of serving in love, integrity, humility, patience, forgiveness, stewardship, empathy, healing, and community building.

No input from me, but according to Ephesians 2:10; *"For we are God's handiwork, created in Christ Jesus to do good works, which God prepared in advance for us to do"*. I now reflect that this work was not for my brother or my parents, it was for me. My brother and I had similar childhood experiences, we enjoyed travelling, music, and food but he died at the age of 27 years. His work was finished, and mine had just started. Greenleaf in his book, The Servant as Leader said:

"The servant is fully human. The servant leader is functionally superior because he is closer to the ground – he hears things, sees things, and his intuitive insight is exceptional. Because he is dependable and trusted" (pg. 43)

This quote struck a chord in me, but was I fully human? At the end of my first degree in 1999 at the Houston Community College System in Houston Texas, we were asked in one of our classes to write these four words on a note card: START, STOP,

BEGIN and CONTINUE. The professor further explained that to each of these words we commit to ourselves the thing/s as we progress in life; we would either carry or leave according to the word on the line. I have not been as good as I had hoped but that postcard is still in my wallet today as a reminder and every now and then I commit to begin again. See picture inserted:

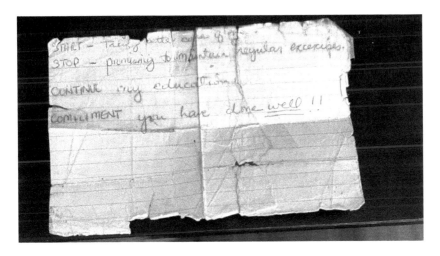

Commencement is the beginning and the end; how unique in definition this word became a part of my life as it was revealed to me. What I gained in practice through experiential occurrences enhanced my learning journey as a follower finding refuge designed to supply real-life examples of love in action. I was taken advantage of as a child, student, young woman, entrepreneur, wife, and mother.

Yet the desire to rebel and to make those who hurt me pay back all they had stolen was not moving quickly. All I continued to want to see manifested in their lives healing, deliverance, improvement, and excellence. LOVE makes your response unfamiliar to those whose motives are to destroy.

According to Ephesians 2:10; "For we are God's handiwork, created in Christ Jesus to do good works, which God prepared in advance for us to do." I am proud to say that with the mantle as a servant leader caused me to pivot, and activate what lie dormant, and illuminated my worth. The price I paid was enough to cover the expense owed by my future inheritors for generations. No, I am not Jesus Christ, but I learned invaluable lessons that will remain with me throughout my life and will become a legacy that others will emulate.

Our positions in life often reveal that to serve others you must be proven. What do I mean by that? I endured tragedies and suffered many traumatic experiences but my call to serve others outweighed the charges levied against me. I was a victim in my state as a leader, defending myself was not an option; the defense was already done for me in advance. Such incidents left wounds and bruises unsterilized and not healed. While in many instances mental health erosion and one's ability to function remained stifled.

I needed to go to therapy. I have researched therapist, but time for me has proven that scars are a necessary armor of a warrior. I have invited the one who is the counselor of all therapists, the Holy Spirit to abide and exist at my address. In return His abundant supply of Grace has made me more equipped for the task. I credit my sanity to the one who makes all things new, Jesus Christ. I buried my pain in tears at his feet, and in true fatherly posture he always comes to my defense. I could not fathom seeing the demise of my heritage due to the lack of knowledge, and the avalanche of ignorance.

The severity of not responding as a servant leader exposes the lack of love, compassion, and community. The New Living translation implores us to do this in Romans 12:2- "Do not copy the behavior and customs of this world, but let God transform you into a new person by changing the way you think. Then you will learn to know God's will for you, which is good, pleasing, and perfect." Discrimination, prejudice, eviction, and promotion pass up are opportunities for transformation to occur in one's life thus making space for the Holy Spirit to intervene and supply insight, direction, and comfort.

The writings of Hebrews and Jeremiah, exclaims Hebrews 8: 7-8 (NLT)," *If the first covenant had been faultless, there would have been no need for a second covenant to replace it. 8. But when God found fault with the people, he said: "The day is coming, says the Lord, when I will make a new covenant with the people of Israel and Judah."* Covenant is a commitment, one that God never defaults on even from old, Jeremiah 31: 33b- 34(NLT)" ... *I will put my instructions deep within them, and I will write them on their hearts. I will be their God, and they will be my people. [34] And they will not need to teach their neighbors, nor will they need to teach their relatives, saying, 'You should know the LORD.'*

LESSONS LEARNED

"For it is God who works in you to will and to act in order to

fulfill his good and purpose," Philippians 2:13

The qualities becoming after being transformed in life as an individual and leader signifies the assurance that the journey is possible. The experiences though full of trauma, oppression, depression, drama, constant therapy, and many prayers often saw LOVE and Grace present through all of it. Constantly, I faced negative feedback that indicated that my efforts would go unrecognized as my presence was not welcomed. Instinctively, such moments opened the doors to allow scripture to provide solace in every trial that I faced.

"No weapon formed against me shall prosper; and EVERY tongue

that shall rise against thee in judgment thou shalt condemn. This is

the heritage of the servants of the LORD, and their righteousness",

Isaiah 54:17.

I became tough after a while, after all my life has been fumbled many times over, my steps at intervals weak in performance, but amazingly in that while I was being fumbled, God kept me from hitting or staying on the ground and instead picked me up through the unction of his Holy Spirit.

Although a baby girl was born some fifty plus years ago to working class (immigrant) parents, she was destined for more, and the assignment was HUGE, but she could handle it. Moreover, if Nehemiah in his assignment to restore Jerusalem, faced opposition, and kept focus and was victorious. I decided that I could and would win. As a substitute teacher, I often reminded students that though life threw them insidious curve balls, who they are was chosen before they were born. Indicative of the words penned by Jeremiah 1:5, "*I knew you before I formed you in your mother's womb. Before you were born, I set you apart and appointed you as my prophet to the nations.*" Therefore, it was incumbent for me to see it through once I realized that my life had a purpose.

In each stage of life, there was formulation of strategy, circumstance, and events which did not align with each other making the journey unpredictable. I learned to be content in all, not an easy lesson learned, but one I learned from the scripture found in Philippians 4:11. I was determined to create a space in my life and my own life path that I would make a difference. Through every step, I took a chance to give more than I received and serve while healing.

In each lesson, the radiance of God's power hovered over my decisions to continue with caution, I was being groomed as a leader, albeit transformational in nature, but servant in heart. But, I did not recognize it. I knew that some of the places where I landed, the standards were below average, as it seemed that at every turn I had to fight.

Lingering in the desire to engage and retaliate towards my enemies became fainter as time progressed. This was not a fair process to my flesh, but it was an opportunity for God to shape me for his purpose. Too many lessons to learn and not enough respect while being a pupil. Accordingly, Matthew 20:27 implores us "*to become slaves if we wish to be first*". Each chapter during the transition magnified the characteristics of being a servant leader:

Listen, Empathize, Healing, Awareness, Persuasion, Conceptualization, Foresight, Stewardship, Commitment to the Growth of people, and Building Community

In reluctance I grew up; I stepped up to the plate as a leader in unusual situations and fostered leadership qualities that transcended throughout my life. I was forced to commit and endure challenging occurrences not designed for me throughout stages of my life but thrived on resources deployed to ensure that I arrived at the destination of my assignments. I never stopped learning but used acceptance avoidance to mitigate through channels making changes beneficial to growth. Leading while bleeding is not popular but is most profitable and the results are always outstanding when God is the center of what you choose to do. I learned each lesson laced with LOVE, integrity, humility, listening, empathy, stewardship, and forgiveness.

Love

"The faithful love of the Lord never ends! His mercies never cease." Lamentations 3:22 ~NLT

Love is a sacrifice, and despite how you feel emotionally about someone, to love them when they frustrate you, and make choices that affect your peace is not sexy. Often the song written by Hezekiah comes to mind when loving the unlovable.

"I need you; you need me! We are all apart of God's body, stand with me agree with me, we are all apart of God's body. It is his will that every need be supplied. You are important to me. I need you to survive." (Hezekiah Walker)

As a leader in any form in all aspects you must prove to others the grace to which love covers. Leading in love is supposed to come with the territory while being a leader, often it is particularly challenging. Love is existential despite the circumstances, what most people do not realize or discover is that love comes in various forms and packages, and not just from the people we expect. God always has a person who is fighting for you in your corner, praying you through a situation. The evidence that love exists is an example of when you do not fail, continue to stand, and persevere even in your darkest moments.

Integrity

"So, stop telling lies. Let us tell our neighbors the truth, for we are all parts of the same body." Ephesians 4:25~NLT

Nothing could be more distasteful than having to deal with an individual who is not honest, and truthful. Integrity makes an ugly person become extremely beautiful to the eyes. Having no integrity discredits whatever contributions in other areas that you may be qualified. My entire life I served people whose values did not align with integrity, and I had to disconnect myself from them. Integrity provides a level of trust, even with people who do not necessarily support your vision or goals.

Humility

"Always be humble and gentle. Be patient with each other, making allowance for each other's faults because of your love." Ephesians 4:2~NLT

Being approachable, friendly, and non-controversial is an asset, especially in leadership. There will be times when being critical to obtain a goal is useful, but this is not always the case. Hopefully, the extent to which individuals are called to lead demands that humility is ever present. Grace, empathy, and forgiveness are easy to extend when you are walking in humility and attributable to ensuring that peace continues to exist within.

Empathy

"These are just the beginning of all that he does, merely a whisper of his power. Who, then, can comprehend the thunder of his power?" Job 26: 14 ~NLT

Being empathetic ordinarily was always a challenge for me, as I have an A-type personality and work ethic. While the sentiments of sympathy come easy, being empathetic is in my interpretation more involved. Not all people are genuine in their needs and are hypocritical to the process that makes empathy a beacon. Yet empathy requires individuals to be compassionate, and jubilant at the drop of a hat. Therefore, empathy is not cyclical to one's personality type; it is more likely to show up in others of a softer monotone.

Stewardship

"Now go up into the hills, bring down timber, and rebuild my house. Then I will take pleasure in it and be honored, says the Lord." Haggai 1:18~NLT

When people see the word stewardship, it is at once associated with finances. Stewardship is about being accountable in any relationship, transaction, and role responsibility. The presence of "stewardship" motivates individual/s to see value in others and help them to achieve beyond their own sight. Being a good steward ensures that legacy will continue, and generations' lives are transformed because of your unselfish sacrifices. Stewardship demands care, and introspection.

Listen

"Listen to me; listen and pay close attention." Isaiah

28:23~NLT

Listening is different from communication or effective otherwise. It was a difficult lesson for me because I like to talk, until my son had to correct me on a matter especially important to him that I missed. The lessons learned cost me, fiscally, emotionally, and physically. Sometimes we are unable to provide people with respect but being committed to hearing them out, and being able to acknowledge that you heard them in most cases brings satisfaction and joy. Another vital aspect of listening is feedback. Feedback supplies empowerment and disqualifies mystical thoughts to its receivers.

Community Building

"Now I say to you that you are Peter (which means rock), and upon this rock I will build my church, and the powers of hell will not conquer it." Matthew 16:18~NLT

Legacy lies in community building, it is important to the future generations, and to the future of a nation. My parents were community builders, and my brother and I often found ourselves involuntarily completing community acts because we were derivatives in the relationship. Leaders should always seek to transfer, hopefully positive, knowledge gained to others, especially when it will do well. Transparency in community building also has a role, once everyone is clear on what to expect and what is expected in their respective roles; expect to reap rewards beneficial to society.

Forgiveness

"Create in me a clean heart, O God. Renew a loyal spirit within me." Psalms 51:10~NLT

There is much to be upset about from my writing, but not enough to keep me in isolation for the rest of my life. Each of these lessons propelled me to move forward, and to acknowledge that a price was paid for my ignorance, so too must I release those who have done me wrong in the journey the same grace extended to me. The bible explains in Psalms 78:39, *"that we are but flesh, and in it dwells no good thing."* More importantly, I learned that forgiveness is for me.

AS I CLOSE…

In my life, the impact of leadership change span decades, commencing from kindergarten to adult hood, encountering many pit stops and destinations, encompassing love and grace in each moment. Most memorable were the moments when adversity seemed as if it had a chokehold on me and it felt like I would not make it to another day. Until one day I encountered the scripture found in Ephesians 3:20," *Now all glory to God, who is able, through his mighty power at work within us, to accomplish infinitely more than we might ask or think.*" Hope was birth, and the assumption that help was an option made me realize that I could carry the mantle placed on my life. What I discovered in the journey were the lessons that I will take with me and use as a motivation to help other to be transformed.

In my quest to discover and explore servant leadership, while the approaches are similar to servant leadership, my experiences are definitely aligned with being a transformational leader. Servant leadership is not specific to geography, genre or species. It shows up where, when, how and for whoever needs it. So, to those who are brave, bold, and strong to walk, live, and love, I salute you! For it is in those times Jude reminds in chapter 1: 24- 25:

"Now all glory to God, who is able to keep you from falling away and will bring you with great joy into his glorious presence without a single fault. All glory to him who alone is God, our Savior through Jesus Christ our Lord. All glory, majesty, power, and authority are his before all time, and in the present, and beyond all time! Amen"

APPENDIX

CAMPAIGN SPEECH 2016

Good evening PNP'S and good evening lovely people of the Constituency of the Bight! I stand proud as your representative tonight and after December 15, 2016, shouting loud and wide that indeed this is the best constituency and the best people reside here, the Bight!

My faith in God, prayers and your continued support have gotten us through these last 4 years and for this I give God all the praise and thanks. My Bight people, you have been my source of inspiration since day 1 when I decided to run for office, and you continue to be it today. Tirelessly we have worked together to ensure that we became stronger as a community, resilient as a people and more aware of our potential and what lies ahead of us. We are better prepared to embrace our FUTURE together as we take this country with the Progressive National Party to the NEXT LEVEL! WE have been chosen as the first constituency to kick off the official campaign rally, that to me speaks volumes that in the Bight, we know how to do things RIGHT! The constituency, where things are born, created, and innovations are acted on. WE have evolved over the last 4 years together creating partnerships and alliances.

In 2012 when I came to you,

I promised that I would build on and empower you through 4 mean areas:

1. *Rebuilding our communities*
2. *Partnering for Investment*
3. *Fostering Entrepreneurship*
4. *Preserving Environment*

I am proud to say that with your help we have achieved this and more. Tirelessly our communication and the pulse of your government have been felt through private partnerships, community outreach and your participation. Over the last 4 years we have increased community involvement for our seniors, our children, and for families with government and private partnership participation. Private partnership yielded clean streets, garbage bins, community cleanups, community givebacks, employment, additional beach access parking, and scholarships all to rebuild our communities. I am proud to say that many of you embraced the opportunity, and some of you are still working on it. Your trust in me has been phenomenal over these last 4 years and I am asking for your support again; to be the voice for you in parliament, on the streets of Turks and Caicos and internationally on the world scene. I am proud of you! My Bight people you are my rock!

Partnering for Investment suffered some setbacks but your support to keep the fire going is what drives me to continue supporting these partnerships aiming to provide multiple opportunities for employment for you. But there are many smaller projects happening within the Bight constituency that are gradually moving and will be in full bloom 2017 and beyond. We cannot improve on our community without involvement/partnership from others, and the government has seen it fit to return bodies that will help you to become full partners in all things Turks and Caicos through entities such as the Center for Entrepreneurial Development and Invest TCI. These bodies were created to assist you in advancing economically through small businesses making your mark in the Tourism industry.

It is no more than fair for you to be an active participant in the economy of the Turks and Caicos as your constituency drives the Turks and Caicos Islands position and rating on the world travel, and financial market. Many of you are still in the development stage of your business whilst some of you are in full gear and full speed ahead capitalizing on the opportunities. Overall, your strides have encouraged me, and this will continue to be a part of my commitment and mandate to you. With this I pledge the fostering of entrepreneurship will continue in 2016 and beyond.

You continue to make us all proud, playing your part in the Environment by keeping your surroundings and adhering to notices provided by the other stakeholders, but overall supporting your pride of cleanliness as Bightian and a Turks and Caicos Islander! You are evolving as you play your part!

My people of the Bight Constituency, we are not changing now, and we are not turning back now! We are moving forward to the next level! We are moving forward with the Progressive National

Party! We are moving forward with a team which has proven that it can, and it will choose wisely for our country, its citizens, and our guests! There is no turning back for us me and I invite you my people to on election day to send a clear message to my opponents that a Progressive National Party candidate, and team members is the only choice for your vote on Election Day December 15, 2016. This party has sacrificed a lot in these past years but hard work, and perseverance prevailed.

My people there is no turning back now, my plans for you are not limited to but include the following:

A community office opening to address the community concerns daily and efficiently. Expressed office hours that are in line with your needs. phase 2 of the multi-recreational centers. Yes, you heard right centers there will be a full and complete center next to where we stand, and full green space park in the Bosco Chan area; and Eco - friendly recreational center in Juba Sound.

1. *The Center for Entrepreneurial Development is already open and operative. I intend to ensure that we receive more than our full share of engagement from this center teaching and*

training all of you to take part in the economy of our country

positively and for the growth of small business owners. We

shall and we will be a part of an ever-growing Turks and

Caicos Islands.

2. *These first four years we in the Bight have seen that we were*

   not excluded from institutional change and upgrades. WE

   saw the building of a new high school in Long Bay Hills that

   sits in the Bight! Closer to home and ultramodern! 2 phases

   down and 1more to go! Our landmark, icon school received

   upgrades and new bathrooms all to enhance our

   constituency. This is only the beginning; I have already

   lobbied for and will continue to until completion of 2 green

   fitness parks to help youth development in sports! In addition

   to government grants and scholarships received by some of

   the constituents of the Bight, through government help, I wish

   to invite private partners to continue giving, as I look to

   address the students who are not academically inclined, and

   address the needs of technical, vocational areas so

   desperately needed in our country. Constituents of the Bight,

I will continue to support the policy of the Minister of Education and advocate your place to ensure that you are always a part of the plan.

I will continue to be a part of the national conversation on Crime and will contribute to the solutions in which to reduce the occurrence of such. I pledge to support programs that will offer rehabilitation for offenders of drugs, alcohol, gambling, and violent abuse. I will support programs that offer urban renewal and social improvements for all residents of the Bight whose income does not meet the basic needs of each household. I pledge to be supportive of Turks and Caicos Islands supporting and reaching Higher Class of living, owning, and employing; I am supportive of lower income persons moving from low -to middle class income status. I pledge to serve this our country, our Turks, and Caicos faithfully! The Bight, I pledge to be your voice once again, I pledge to continue to take this country to the NEXT LEVEL! I PLEDGE TO TAKE YOU MY PEOPLE OF THE BIGHT TO THE NEXT LEVEL! There is no turning back now, we have no time to concentrate on only one area, I pledge to address all areas. Everything that affects us as a people I pledge to support DEMOCRACY! In doing this, I ask you to Vote for the PNP! Vote for all the candidates, all 15 of the PNP! Vote for me, Porsha Stubbs Smith! ED#6. Return this progressive government back to office!

CAMPAIGN GOALS 2012

Committed to Build, Foster, and Preserve with a Vision to further Advance our People.

- Building our community
- Vision for Sound Development
- Fostering Entrepreneurship
- Preserving our Environment

Party Top 5 Accomplishments to achieve: 2012

Top 5 Accomplishments

- Manifesto Objectives
- Dept/Ministry Objectives
- Improve Community Partnerships
- Infrastructure Advancement
- Engage Corporate and Social Responsibility

Constituency Accomplishments

- Foster partnership with constituency stakeholder (partnership - Scotiabank, Beaches TCI, Island Hoops, and others)

- Lower Bight - Vendor Craft Market upgrade (Beaches, TCI)

- Community Upgrade and Renewal

- Advocate more Parking Space at beach access (Forbes Road)

- Advocate more Lights installed in communities

- Advocate new Road Construction

- Community Meetings and Involvement

- Support more private scholarships advocated through community partners

- Engage young entrepreneurs

- Empower Community Cleanliness and Environmental standards

Ministry of Environment and Home Affairs

- Dog Ordinance Amendments

- Fire fees and allows amendments

- Taxi Drivers Fees Increase

- Turtles Project

- Fortis (Middle Caicos) Subsidy

Ministry of Health and Human Services

- Coordinate 5 Ambulances to islands

- Train 22 Emergency Responders

- Vector Control Trucks (North Caicos, Grand Turk, and Provo)

- Complete the framework regarding the Health Strategic Plan

- Commence the framework for the Healthcare Renewal Strategy

- Progress the work of 2 clinics - Salt Cay and Middle Caicos

- Commence the work on the Tobacco Legislation

- Commence the capital project program Mental Health Home (Wellness Center Grand Turk)

- Special Needs Reform (create registry and introduce more services, additional resources provided)

- Formalization of Contract Management Unit Hospital

- Complete Financial and Clinical Audit of the Hospital

- Improve Primary Healthcare offerings making more services available in the community

Tourism Environment Culture Gaming & Heritage

- Fish Fry - Grand Turk

- New Flights and Routes (British Airways, United Airlines, Jet Blue, Expanded American Airlines Service)

- National Parks Ordinance - Amendment

- Complete Gaming Policy

- Heritage Capital Projects - pending

- Fisheries Regulations - Amendment

- Removal of Mega One Triton (pending)

- Culture Ordinance - Repeal

- Historic Wrecks Regulations - Amendment

- The Bight Fish fry and Cultural Market - pending

NEW PROJECTS - Completed in the Bight by TCIG

- Long Bay High School

- New Bathrooms - Ianthe Pratt Primary School

Vision 2016 - Re - Election

TRUSTED, PROVEN, COMMITTED and DEDICATED LEADER!

- SERVANT LEADERSHIP

- MENTOR ENTREPRENEURSHIP

- RECREATIONAL DEVELOPMENT

- INFRASTRUCTURE ADVANCEMENT

References

Burns, J. (1978). *Leadership* . New York, NY : Harper & Row.

Greenleaf, R. K. (1991, 2008). *The Servant as Leader.* Atlanta:
The Greenleaf Center for Servant Leadershp.

Hess, H. (1956). *The journey to the East* . London, UK: P.Owen .

Moskala, J. (2014). The Historical Books . In S. Bell, *Servants and
Friends A Biblical Theology of Leadership* (pp. 65-69).
Springs, MI: Andrews University Press .

Northouse, P. G. (2019). *Leadership: theory and practice, Ed:8th.*
Thousand Oaks, CA: SAGE.

Piaget, J. (1932). *The Moral Judgment of the Child* . London :
Routledge & Kegan Paul .

Prevention, C. f. (2023, September 18). CDC. Preventing multiple
forms of violence: A strategic vision for connecting the
dots [PDF - 775 KB]. 2016. Atlanta , GA , USA .

Ricciardi, J. A. (2014). To lead is to love: An exploration into the
role of love in leadership (Order No. 3583436). *Available*

from ProQuest Dissertations & Theses Global; ProQuest

One Academic. (1560246500). Retrieved from

https://www.proquest.com/disser-theses/lead-is-love-

exploration-into-role-leadership/docview/1560246500/se-2.

Printed in the USA
CPSIA information can be obtained
at www.ICGtesting.com
LVHW022008310124
770461LV00009B/234